ARABS,
TURKS,
AND
PERSIANS

Library of Congress Control Number: 2024947161

ISBN (paperback): 978-1-963271-45-4
ISBN (Ebook): 978-1-963271-46-1

AFPC Press
American Foreign Policy Council
509 C Street NE
Washington, DC 20002

Published by Armin Lear Press, Inc.
215 W Riverside Drive, #4362
Estes Park, CO 80517

ARABS, TURKS, AND PERSIANS

Geopolitics and Ideology
in the Greater Middle East

SVANTE E. CORNELL

AFPC

CONTENTS

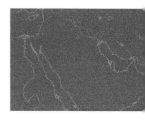

INTRODUCTION

For decades, the Greater Middle East has been a leading challenge to American foreign policy. This vast region – ranging from North Africa in the west to Afghanistan in the east, and from the borders of Central Asia down to the Horn of Africa in the south – has been a cauldron of turmoil that has affected not just American interests, but generated threats to the American homeland.

Reasons for U.S. engagement in this region have been plentiful. Part of World War Two was fought in North Africa, and the U.S. soon after identified the Gulf's oil reserves as crucial to America's interests. The region was the scene also for America's confrontation with the Soviet Union during the Cold War. From the 1970s onward, Islamist ideology began to play a key role across the region. At times, the U.S. benefited from this to counter communism as in Afghanistan; but increasingly the U.S. found itself a target of the more extreme forms of Islamist ideology.

The multitude of challenges in this region has led to some confusion. What should be the focus of U.S. policy in the Greater

Middle East? Opinions vary. Some adamantly claim that the conflict between Israel and the Palestinian Arabs is the cauldron that determines the future of the region and should take precedence. Others focus on the ambitions of the Islamist regime in Iran to assert hegemony over the region. Still others contend that Sunni extremism of the Al Qaeda or ISIS variety is the leading threat. At different times, these and other approaches have all dominated U.S. foreign policy. After 1979, the challenge posed by the Iranian regime and its millenarian ideology loomed large. But Iraq's invasion of Kuwait led to the policy of "dual containment" of the two powers. Meanwhile, the U.S continued to rely on close ties with Saudi Arabia, even though the Kingdom was a chief source of the Salafi-Jihadi extremism that would give birth to Al Qaeda. The September 11 attacks on the United States understandably led Washington to focus primarily on the Sunni Jihadi threat. However, this led to some confusion regarding Iran: Increasingly, some began to argue that since Iran also opposed Sunni extremism, perhaps America and Iran could find an accommodation of sorts.

Lately, the case has been made that the U.S. has focused too much on this region, to the detriment of other priorities. In this view, this is a region that only embroils America in arcane conflicts in which the U.S. has no stake. The U.S. gets manipulated by highly problematic partners and gets pulled into Middle Eastern conflicts. Its presence in turn helps create resentment that fuels the very threats it then has to waste finite resources to confront. Furthermore, since America is increasingly energy-independent and some believe the world is moving away from a reliance on fossil fuels, the region will not matter as much to America in the future as it did in the past. As a result, the U.S. should seek to extricate itself from a central role in the region and help create an order in which the regional powers of the Greater Middle East can themselves manage the region.

The region certainly needs management. In the past few decades, major shifts have taken place that have rearranged the geopolitics across the Greater Middle East. Some of these shifts have resulted from U.S. action, and others from processes internal to the region. In sum, key Arab powers have seen their role as regional powers collapse, while the power of non-Arab states has risen. The U.S. invasion of Iraq in 2003 obliterated the regional standing of one of the main Arab military powers, turning it into a client state in which America and Iran fought for influence. Then, the Arab upheavals of 2011 led to the downfall of Egypt and Syria, also major Arab powers. In the Arab world, this allowed Saudi Arabia and small but infinitely wealthy Gulf monarchies like the UAE and Qatar to emerge as power-brokers in the Arab world.

Meanwhile, the region's traditional non-Arab powers – Turkey and Iran – stepped in to fill the void. Iran had initially been seriously alarmed by the U.S. invasions of Afghanistan and Iraq in 2001-2003, fearing that it would be next in line. But as America's fortunes in both countries declined, Iran gradually stepped in to take advantage of the turmoil in Iraq. Tehran also came to see the benefit of the U.S. removing neighboring governments that were threatening to Iran's interests and putting U.S. forces in a place Iran could attack through its proxies. Following the Arab upheavals, it intensified is efforts to build what we will call an "Arc of Domination" across the region, ranging from Yemen in the east to Syria and Lebanon in the west – providing the Iranian regime with direct access to the Mediterranean and a vantage point to strike at Israel from southern Syria.

Turkey's entry into Middle Eastern geopolitics was an equally significant factor. The Ottoman Empire had been the overlord of large parts of the Arab world, but from the 1920s onward the Turkish republic had oriented itself westward, vowing to avoid entanglement in the "backward" Middle East. Certainly, Turkey had been part of the American alliance system and thus a core part of the Baghdad Pact and CENTO. But its key interests lay elsewhere. With the end of the Cold War, however, Ankara gradually began to involve itself in Middle Eastern affairs, mainly as a result of perceived threats emanating from the region. The rise of Islamist politics to the fore with Recep Tayyip Erdogan would change the calculus, however. Following the Arab upheavals, Ankara made an aggressive bid for influence across the Middle East and North Africa, involving itself in many of the region's conflicts, including military deployments in Syria, Iraq and Libya as well as the opening of military bases in Qatar and Somalia.

The geopolitics of the Greater Middle East have, like elsewhere, been determined greatly by realist calculations of national interest, coupled with age-old prejudices and personal relations among regional leaders. But it is the contention in this book that ideological elements have been particularly important in this region, alongside these factors. Iran's regime has been the prime mover in the region since 1979, remaking the region's geopolitics by its bold assertion of a revolutionary Islamist agenda that deliberately ignored national boundaries. Everyone was put on the defensive, reacting to Iran. The Saudis promoted their own

Islamism as an answer to Tehran, focused on the Salafi Sunni tradition of the Arabian Peninsula. In Turkey, the ruling military administration of the early 1980s launched the notion of a "Turkish-Islamic" synthesis, which over time would empower Turkish Islamism, itself influenced by the ideology of the Muslim Brotherhood.

If Iran is the "prime mover," the response of the Sunni powers to the Iranian threat is key to the stability of the region. Ironically, they went in opposite directions. The Saudis and most Gulf Emirates had come to realize that their support of Salafism had spiraled out of control, generating forces that threatened their own internal stability. They therefore sought to move toward moderation. But Turkey went the other way: under Erdogan, its foreign policy was animated by an ideologically colored view of the region and an ambition to remake the region in its own image. Predictably, this caused a deep rift in the Sunni world that only benefited Iran.

In recent years, uncertainty concerning America's commitment to the Greater Middle East combined with continued relentless Iranian pressure to lead to a realignment. Turkey and Arab powers appeared to bury the hatchet. While a positive development, it does not change the fact that the stability of the Middle East depends, for the foreseeable future, on the trilateral relationship among Turks, Arabs and Persians.

This book explores this state of affairs and its implications by delving deeper into how the current geopolitics of the Greater Middle East came to be. A first few chapters look back to the history of the region and the historic rivalries among Turks, Arabs and Persians up to the end of the Cold War. Next, we examine the main current power centers of the region – beginning with Iran, followed by Saudi Arabia and Turkey. The book then turns to the geopolitical competition of recent years – looking into Iran's efforts to build an "Arc of Domination" across the region and Turkey's attempt to create a "Brotherhood Axis." We then move to how things have played out as a result – the advance of Islamists following the Arab Upheavals, the civil war among the Sunnis from 2013 to 2018, America's pendulum swings with regard to Iran policy, and the reshuffle of the region following Turkey's turn in a more nationalist direction. The book ends with an attempt to draw out implications for America's approach to the geopolitics of the Greater Middle East.

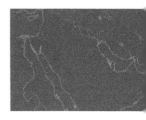

1.
ARABS, TURKS AND PERSIANS AND THE DIVIDED *UMMAH*

In the politics of the Muslim world, the past is very much present, as it is taken as reference to an extent surpassing most other civilizations. The reason lies in a simple but troubling dichotomy. Muslims see Islam as the culmination of the monotheistic tradition, and Muhammad as the last prophet. Furthermore, soon after the prophet's death, Muslims conquered enormous swathes of lands, and gave birth to a civilization that rapidly came to lead the world in terms of the advancement of science. In the past several centuries, by contrast, the picture has been very different. The core Muslim lands – understood here as those dominated by Arab, Persian and Turkic peoples – experienced a long decline that put them at a disadvantage compared to European powers, whose dominance was followed by America's ascendancy. The result has been a dissonance between a supposedly golden past and a more disappointing present. Not surprisingly, a key focus of debate has centered around two questions: what went wrong, and what to do about this predicament?

To an extent greater than elsewhere, religion plays an important factor in the identification of many Muslims. It is easy for outsiders to dismiss the notion of an *Ummah*, a Muslim community, given the amount of bloodshed Muslims committed against each other virtually from the moment Muhammad died. Still, this notion remains a strong factor in the lives of many Muslims, who tend to see foreign co-religionists as brethren to a much larger degree than Christians would. Even living in secular Turkey, the first question strangers most frequently asked this author was, quite simply, "are you Muslim?" When Muslims think of the *Ummah*, they think of an idealized notion of a Muslim community that never existed. But like any imagined community, this ideal has political relevance.

The past has also guided the different approaches to dealing with the predicament of Muslim societies. On one end, some have sought emulate the success of the West by embracing the secular nation-state. On the other end, others have rejected this notion entirely, arguing instead for the recreation of the idealized Caliphate that briefly existed after Muhammad's passing. In between, all kinds of ideas of the shaping of state and society have come and gone.

If mythical unity is a factor, so is also the divisions among Muslims. Arabs gradually lost control of the Muslim world, and political and economic power over territories they conquered shifted to Persian and Turkic peoples. The process of conversion took centuries; and the new converts put their own mark on Islam, developing understandings of the religion that were truly Turkic and Persian. In fact, it would be accurate to say that these peoples developed theologies that were suitable to their own national traditions and values – and sometimes their narrow interests. For example, the sixteenth-century Iranian ruler Shah Ismail in large part made Shi'ism the state religion in order to differentiate his realm from the Sunni Ottomans to the west and Uzbeks to the north.

Geopolitical History in the Muslim World

It is a paradox that the rapid expansion of the early Arab empire led it to become progressively less Arab. This was not yet a significant issue during Muhammad's lifetime, because his realm remained limited to the Arabian Peninsula. His four successor caliphs, however, oversaw the conquest of Iraq and the Levant, Iran, eastern Turkey, the Caucasus and Egypt. During the early Umayyad dynasty, this was followed by the conquest of Central Asia including Afghanistan, Pakistan up to the Indus, as well as the Maghreb. Suddenly, Arabs were a small minority of the population. They initially remained a majority of the *Muslim* population, but this soon changed as a result of conversion. Aside from whatever appeal the new religion may have had, conversion was convenient because it absolved the population from the payment of the *jiziya* tax imposed upon the conquered peoples, and led to higher social status. Within a relatively short time, the Arabs became a minority even among the Muslims of the empire. At least initially, most of these non-Arab Muslims were of Persianate stock. They were originally treated as a separate class of "clients" of the Arab clans, but gradually demanded to have equal status to the Arabs and found ammunition for this view in the religion of Islam.

This helped spur the Abbasid revolt, led by an Arab family that drew support among disgruntled Arab clans, the Shi'a faction, as well as the non-Arab Muslims. By 750, the Abbasids had routed the reigning Umayyads and moved to establish a new capital at Baghdad. Two centuries later, the Abbasid Caliphate was effectively taken over by the Buyids, a Shi'a Persian dynasty, which nevertheless left the Abbasid Caliph as a religious figurehead. Thus, Arab control over the Muslim empire essentially ended by the end of the first Millennium AD. The shape of the modern Greater Middle East then began to take shape, because the Persian rule of the Buyids collapsed in the mid-eleventh century as the Turkic Seljuks swept in and established control over Baghdad and the empire. Following the example of the Buyids, the Seljuks left the Abbasid Caliphate in place. It would only formally expire with the Mongol invasion of 1258.

The Mongols ruled over much of the Middle East and Iran, and the Seljuks retreated into Anatolia. There, they would soon be replaced by a new powerful dynasty, that of the Ottomans. Meanwhile, further south, another Turkic dynasty – the Mamluks – ruled over Egypt and the Levant. While the Mamluks maintained the status of the Arabic language, the ruling class retained their separate ethnic identity and continued to speak Turkish among themselves. Mamluk rule would continue until they were defeated by their fellow Turkic cousins, the Ottomans, in the early sixteenth century. Iran also fell under the rule of various Turkic dynasties following the collapse of Mongol rule, culminating in the emergence of the Safavid dynasty in the sixteenth century.

Turks appeared on the ascendant everywhere, but were a minority ruling over multinational empires.

After the Ottomans disposed of the Mamluks, the Ottoman Sultans laid claim to the Islamic Caliphate. Although the Mongols had killed the last Abbasid Caliph, the Mamluks had found an escapee relative they placed as Caliph in order to shore up their religious legitimacy. The Ottomans then claimed the title on the theory that it belonged to them after their conquest of Egypt. This was part of a claim of legitimacy over the leadership of Sunni Islam. Meanwhile, the similarly Turkic Safavids differentiated themselves by making the Shi'a branch the state religion of Iran. For several centuries, the Sunni Turks and Shi'a Iranians would struggle for supremacy over the mainly Arab lands of the core Middle East; control over these lands mainly remained with the Turks, with brief interludes of Iranian rule.

Until well into the twentieth century, thus, there was no independent Arab state. In Arabia, the antecedents of the present Saudi dynasty staged a first rebellion against the Ottomans in 1801, but only lasted for a decade before being put down. Egypt would also assert its autonomy from Ottoman rule in the early nineteenth century; but this happened under the rule of Muhammad Ali, an ethnic Albanian originally appointed by the Ottoman Sultan. Egypt then fell under British rule. Only in the early twentieth century did Arab nationalism begin to become a factor. Following the Ottoman defeat in World War one, some Arab lands finally gained statehood. The Saud dynasty began to put together the Saudi Kingdom, a process that was completed by 1932. Meanwhile, the British granted Egypt independence in 1922. Other Arab lands fell under French and British mandates, and gained independence during the 1930s or after the second world war.

This history created considerable resentment among Arabs, both against Western powers and Turkish and Iranian overlords. The Turks and Iranians had their own resentments as well: both empires were in serious decline by the eighteenth century. The Ottoman realm shrank gradually following Mehmed IV's siege of Vienna in 1683, and by the early nineteenth century the empire began to lose many of its European possessions. Not staying at that, western powers forced the Ottomans to provide privileges to their citizens living within the empire, through contracts known as "capitulations." This downward trend culminated with the Treaty of Sèvres of 1920, which aimed to partition the Empire into a number of European-controlled sectors, and to create Armenian and Kurdish states in its eastern portions. While this treaty was never implemented because of the Turkish war of independence, it has remained a profound grievance among Turks to this day. It is frequently used to remind Turks of the alleged designs of western powers upon their country. Yet compared to Turkey, Iran fared worse: in the nineteenth century, the country was effectively partitioned into a Russian sphere of interest in the north, and a British one in the south. Russia even incorporated the South Caucasus, large parts of which had been Iranian, into its empire. Russian and Iranian designs on Iran would continue up until the second world war.

In the twentieth century, Turkey and Iran both emerged as functional nation-states and took up their place as regional powers. The Arab world, by contrast, came to be divided into almost two dozen different states, meaning that no true Arab nation-state has come into being. Perhaps this was never a realistic possibility given the broad geography of Arab-speaking peoples and the many significant differences between them. In the absence of a unified Arab nation, several candidates emerged for leadership in the Arab world. An obvious candidate was Egypt, by virtue of its history and large population. Saudi Arabia built its claim on being the custodian of the holiest sites of Islam, and subsequently on its financial wealth. Iraq and Syria sought leading roles based on radical Arab nationalist ideology and military might. Other Arab countries were too weak and small to contend. Thus emerged the setting for the geopolitical rivalries in the Greater Middle East during the twentieth century, featuring two large non-Arab powers as well as several contenders for Arab leadership. We will return to this geopolitical rivalry in the next chapter. For now, let us turn to the overlap between ethnic division and religious divisions in the Muslim world.

The Divided Ummah: Hanafi, Shia, and Hanbali

Divisions within Islam are a sensitive topic. Muslims tend to stress the unity of the *Ummah*, playing down divisions among them. Islamic theologians have campaigned hard over the past several centuries to downplay differences between the different theological traditions. The argument is that they are all essentially similar, and that divisions among them are exaggerated by foreigners intent on pitting Muslims against each other.

But in fact, these religious divisions are real. They inform the varying perspectives taken by the leading Muslim nations, and very much undergird the prejudices they hold against each other. They also inform their particular claims to leadership of the region. The divide between Sunnis and Shi'a is the best known of these religious differences, but the multiple divides within the Sunni world are no less significant.

The Sunni-Shi'a divide was not, initially, theological but political: The Shi'a argued that the Prophet's son-in-law Ali was the legitimate leader of the *Ummah*. Sunnis disagreed, arguing that the Prophet's companions were equally worthy. Ali, who claimed that Muhammad had anointed him as his heir, was passed over for leadership, and instead the three first caliphs were Muhammad's companions Abu Bakr, Omar and Uthman. When Ali was finally named the fourth Caliph, he faced stiff resistance from within the community, not least from Muhammad's youngest wife Aisha and the governor of Syria, Muawiyah. A civil war among Muslims erupted, known by the euphemism the first "strife" or *fitna*. Ali's standing weakened, and he was eventually murdered in 661, putting an end to the original caliphate. In his place, Muawiyah had himself anointed caliph. He is widely seen to have transformed the Caliphate into a worldly and hereditary kingship, which is why he is not acknowledged among the so-called *Rashidun*, or rightly-guided caliphs, even by Sunnis. Shi'as, on the other hand, revile him and even more so his son and successor Yazid, whom they hold responsible for the killing of Husayn, Ali's son and Muhamad's grandson, at the battle of Karbala in 680. Shi'as commemorate that murder every year by the self-flagellation rituals of *ashura*.

Over time, the political divide came to be religious and to some degree ethnic as well. The biggest difference between Sunnis and Shi'as lies in the organization of the community: Sunni Islam is famously averse to hierarchy, something that has prevented the emergence of unified doctrine; it lacks a formal priesthood. By contrast, even though it lacks a central authority like the Catholic Church and has several centers of authority like Qom and Najaf, Shi'a Islam is organized in a distinctly hierarchical way compared to Sunni Islam, with a dedicated priesthood. Grand Ayatollahs or *marjahs* are at the top, followed by regular Ayatollahs and under them *Hujjat-ul-Islams*. While there were originally few doctrinal differences between Sunnis and Shi'a, multiple minute differences emerged as the two sects developed separately of one another for over a thousand years. The Shi'a further subdivided into several distinct categories, but here we will use the term Shi'a, except when otherwise specified, to refer to the *Jafari* or "twelver" form of Shi'a prevalent in Iran and Iraq, termed thusly because of the belief in a succession of twelve Shi'a imams.

The first Shi'a Muslims were Arabs, and Shi'a communities exist across the Arab world. They form the majority only in Iraq and Bahrain, but minorities persist in practically every Arab country, as well as far beyond in countries like Pakistan and Indonesia. But the dominance of the Shi'a branch in Iran has, in modern times, led to a strong identification of the Shi'a with that country. Particularly after the 1979 revolution, Iran has become the political and theological center of Shi'a Islam globally, notwithstanding the objections and reservations of Iraqi Shi'a clergy. This overlap of national and sectarian divides has become significant in modern-day geopolitics, particularly as Iran has sought to exploit Shi'a minorities in its project to create a sphere of influence in the Greater Middle East.

Meanwhile, the majority Sunnis over time split into distinct schools of jurisprudence and theology. The divisions between these schools in great part follow geographic and ethnic lines that have strengthened the separate identities of Turks and Arabs. The differences may appear arcane, but have considerable relevance for the relative openness of Muslim societies to interaction with the modern world.

The theological divisions concern rather fundamental questions: should holy scripture be followed literally, or should believers be able to interpret the language of the Qur'an according to current societal realities? Do humans have free will, or is their every action predetermined by God? Could humans discern good from evil without the aid of divine revelation? Different answers to these questions have important implications for the outlook on life that prevails in a society.

The debates on these questions in early Muslim history were fiery. Early on, a strongly rationalistic sect called the *Mu'tazilites* developed in the late eighth century. To them, it was obvious that scripture should be read allegorically rather than literally, that humans had free will, and that human reason could tell good from evil without the need of any scripture. They promoted advanced theological arguments to debate a large variety of religious questions. But the *Mu'tazilites* saw heavy pushback from a more austere understanding of the religion. Proponents of the *athari* school of thought, which is the antecedent of today's Salafis, posited that scripture should be accepted in its literal meaning without asking questions. As a result, they opposed the very idea of theology: to them, the very act of engaging in theological debates and reasoning was harmful, because it led believers to depart from the text of scripture. Their answer was simple: read the text. When in doubt, consult the *Sunnah* of the prophet, that is, the recorded sayings and deeds of Muhammad.

Over time, most Muslims came to see both of these extremes as unpractical. The *atharis* were too strict and unreasonable; but the *mu'tazilites* appeared a little too removed from religion. Independently of each other, two ninth century theologians emerged to develop a middle ground. While they opposed the liberal *mu'tazilites*, they used reason and logic to refute *mu'tazilite* theological arguments, as well as those coming from other sects and non-Muslims. These theologians were Mansur al-Maturidi of Samarkand (853-944) and Hasan al-Ashari of Basra (874-936), and they came to be the founders of the two accepted schools of Sunni theology.

Muslim theologians have tried to paper over the difference between these theologians in the interest of promoting "Muslim unity." Yet these two gentlemen took different positions on questions of key importance, for example on the concept of reason and human ability to discern right from wrong independent of divine revelation. Al-Ashari outright rejected such a possibility because he saw it as a direct affront to God's omnipotence. He argued that something is right or wrong only because God ordered it to be so. If humans could decide what is right, that would violate God's omnipotence. Following this logic, Ashari argued that all acts undertaken by men are created by God. Consequently, there are no laws of nature, because that notion would, again, deny the omnipotence of God. To illustrate, the highly influential eleventh-century Asharite scholar Hamid al-Ghazali stated that fire does not cause cotton to burn. That may appear to humans to be a natural law but in fact, it is only God that leads the cotton to burn; and if God decides that it will not happen, it will not. Needless to say, the implications of this type of thinking are far-reaching. As Robert Reilly has argued, the Ashari belief in the total omnipotence of God essentially led his many followers to deny reality, causation, and the meaning of any scientific inquiry. The wide spread of these essentially nihilistic ideas goes a long way to explaining the decline of scientific inquiry in the Muslim world, which Reilly puts as the title of his book: *The Closing of the Muslim Mind.*[1]

Maturidi, by contrast, accepted the notion of man as a rational being, the only created being "who reflects on and understands" the wisdom of God.[2] While Maturidi acknowledged that God is omnipotent, he also argued that God holds himself to the norms he has himself created, and therefore there is a stable and intelligible system of norms. Because God has established such a system, and humans have the capacity to understand God's wisdom, humans can also learn to understand that system. This perspective, unlike the Ashari view, is fully compatible with the pursuit of modern science and rational inquiry.

These theological distinction are replicated in the divergence among the Sunni schools of jurisprudence, which became quite important given the importance of *Sharia,* Islamic law, in Muslim societies. The key question is the extent to which there are other sources of law than the Qur'an and the Sunnah. The more austere interpretations, preferred by the *atharis* and the modern-day Salafis, essentially deny this. Their view came to

---

1   Robert R. Reilly, *The Closing of the Muslim Mind,* Wilmingon, DE: ISI Books, 2011, p. 85.
2   Ulrich Rudolph, *Al-Maturidi and the Development of Sunni Theology in Samarqand,* trans. Rodrigo Adem, Leiden: Brill, 2015, p. 297.

dominate the Hanbali school of jurisprudence, prevalent in the Arabian Peninsula.

Others are less definitive, because the Qur'an hardly provides clear guidance on every matter. Leading Islamic jurists therefore accepted other sources of law. Among them were the consensus of scholars, analogical reasoning, as well as in a subordinate role, local customs and the discretion of jurists. The boldest in embracing such subordinate sources of law is the Hanafi school, founded by Abu Hanifa, an eighth-century scholar of Persianate origin. The Hanafi school – which mostly follows Maturidi's theology – cautions not to focus too rigidly on the strict and literal application of texts, and urges instead consideration for the spirit of the teachings of the religion, and maintains concern for the public interest. Abu Hanifa introduced the notion of the discretion of jurists, in order to ease hardship and apply tolerance and moderation to rulings. (Abu Hanifa did not go as far as the Shi'a, who formally include reason as a specific source of law.)

While the Hanbali and Hanafi schools are two extremes, the Shafi'i and Maliki schools lie somewhere in between. However, the Shafi'i school, which follows Ashari's theology, tends to be in agreement with the Hanbalis on key matters, although it does not take literalism to the same lengths.

Thus, it is possible to identify three basic traditions within the Sunni Islamic world today. A fourth, the rationalistic *mu'tazilite* school, is out of favor. Unfortunately, their archnemesis, the purist *atharis*, stand strong in the shape of the modern-day Salafis, who have dominated the Arabian Peninsula and made inroads across the Muslim world and in immigrant Muslim communities in the West. The restrictive Ashari theology and the Shafi'i school of jurisprudence dominates most Arab lands outside the Arabian Peninsula. By contrast, the Maturidi theology and its companion, the more liberal Hanafi school of jurisprudence dominates in present-day Turkey, the Balkans, and Central Asia – roughly speaking, the areas historically dominated by Turkic peoples. This is also where esoteric forms of Islam known as Sufism, which emphasize a mystic communion with God, are the most widespread. It should be noted, however, the Sufism – although inherently heterodox – is not a friend of rationality. Quite to the contrary, the effort to seek mystical knowledge stand in bright contrast to resorting to reason. The aforementioned Ghazali – who spearheaded the Asharite rejection of reason – in fact ended up seeking solace in mysticism.

These differences in how various peoples understand Islam have had profound influence on the development of societies. The greater appreciation for the capacities of the human mind led to the greater scientific and cultural advances of Persian and Turkic civilization, while the rejection of such led the Arab world, and particularly the Arabian Peninsula, to remain an intellectual backwater. It also means that for all the talk of common Muslim identity, it does not take a long stay in Muslim countries to see that how Turks, Arabs and Persians practice their religion varies greatly; nor does it take long to appreciate that deeply held prejudices and suspicions of each other continue to exist, informed in great part by religious differences.

2.
IDEOLOGY AND RELIGION: THE RISE OF POLITICAL ISLAM

The first half of the twentieth century saw the end of colonialism and the making of the modern Greater Middle East. As Arabs, Turks and Persians took charge of new states, they faced the question how to organize them, and how to orient their foreign policy.

Several facets of this development were remarkable. First, those seeking to enforce Islamic ideas as the basis for the new states were present everywhere, but played only a limited role in the formation of the region's political systems. A number of conservative monarchies emerged that based their legitimacy heavily on religion – in the absence of strong national identities on which the legitimacy of governments could rest. Still, most new political systems tended to borrow from Western ideas. Turkey and Iran were led by secularist and westernizing leaders, while much of the Arab world was dominated by Arab socialism.

Such European ideas were on the ascendancy up until the 1970s, when Islamism began to emerge as a powerful ideological force. Until then, the geopolitical rivalries of the region were relatively manageable, in part because they were subsumed under the global bipolar confrontation between the West and the Soviet bloc. It is a profound irony that Islamism preached the unity of the *ummah*, but that the emergence of Islamism was what led to a rise in geopolitical rivalries within the Greater Middle East.

The following sections will provide a brief overview of the key ideological currents in the Greater Middle East, and the rise of Islamism.

Ideological Trends in the Modern Muslim World

The encounter with the West made the relative decline of the Muslim world blatantly clear. The pronounced differences in power and technological development showed how significant that decline really was – not just compared to some imaginary glory days, but to the rest of the contemporary world. Thus, a variety of thinkers all the way from the Maghreb to the Indian subcontinent developed ideas to bring their homelands out of their decline and to compete with the West. The issues these thinkers focused on were, in one scholar's words, "remarkably invariant:" they related to the relationship between Islam and the rational, empirical sciences; forms of government, including the relationship of religion to politics; national identity and the relationship to the outside world; and the status of women in society.[3]

There was wide consensus that the Muslim world's traditional approach to learning and politics was obsolete. Most focused their ire on the traditional *Ulama*, the Islamic scholars,

---

3   Mansoor Moaddel, *Islamic Modernism, Nationalism, and Fundamentalism: Episode and Discourse*, University of Chicago Press, 2005, p. 7.

and their emphasis on the doctrine of *Taqlid* – imitation or blind following of preceding scholars. It was in terms of the solution to the problem that disagreements emerged. The political ideas that developed can be divided into two key camps: those promoting entirely secular solutions, and those advocating for retaining Islam as the key point of reference. The secular camp further divided into a more liberal group and a more authoritarian one, while the Islamic camp split into modernist and Islamist wings.

Liberal nationalists essentially adopted the Western under-standing of the nation and of liberal democracy. But they did not develop a widespread following. More assertive and authoritarian ideologies proved better prepared to wage the struggle against colonialism and to fill the vacuum left in the turmoil of the post-colonial period. Secular authoritarian nationalists included forces as diverse as the hardline Kemalists in Turkey, the Pahlavi regime in Iran, and Arab socialist movements such as those in Egypt under Nasser, the Baath party in Syria and Iraq, as well as in Algeria. Over time, there were efforts to make these countries more democratic, and in countries like Turkey, Iran and Pakistan, more democratic versions of secular nationalism did advance. But they were squeezed between the retreating authoritarian nation-alists and advancing Islamist forces, both of which were hostile to free inquiry and independent intellectual life.[4]

Islamic modernists, unlike secular nationalists, maintained Islam as their key point of reference. But unlike the Islamists, they sought to reform the ossified understanding of Islamic principles in a progressive direction. One key aim was to reconcile Islam with modernity and science. Islamic modernists remarked that

---

4   Ahmet Kuru, *Islam, Authoritarianism and Underdevelopment: A Global and Historical Compari-son*, Cambridge University Press, 2019.

early Islam was "revolutionary, progressive, liberal and rational," but had succumbed to "stultifying rigidity and reactionary dogmatism."[5] The most influential modernists included Jamaluddin Afghani and especially Muhammad Abduh, who eventually became Chief Mufti of Egypt in the late nineteenth century.[6] Abduh argued that true Islam was fully compatible with reason and science, in fact more so than Christianity. But Islamic modernists like Abduh rejected a separation of religion and politics, arguing this was unnecessary because the Muslim world never faced an institution like the papacy with its claims to temporal power.

Islamic modernists continued to have influence in monarchies like Jordan and Morocco, where Kings with strong traditional Islamic legitimacy adopted their ideas. Similarly, Habib Bourguiba and his successor Zine al-Abidine Ben Ali sought to modernize Tunisia by adopting a version of state-controlled Islamic modernism rather than outright secularism, which they judged inapplicable in an Arab context.[7] But more broadly, Islamic modernist ideas struggled to have widespread political influence.

The Islamists, unlike liberal nationalists, authoritarian nationalists, and Islamic modernists, had no interest in emulating the advances of the West, or to reconcile Islam with reason, science, and modernity. In fact, they rejected modernity and the West entirely, with the possible exception of some technological advances that could prove useful. To the Islamists, the answer lay solely in a full embrace of Islam as an all-encompassing system

5   Pervez Hoodhboy, *Islam and Science: Religious Orthodoxy and the Battle for Rationality*, London: Zed, 1991, p. 55.

6   Mark Sedgwick, *Muhammad Abduh*, London: Oneworld, 2010.

7   Rory McCarthy, "Re-Thinking Secularism in Post-Independence Tunisia," *Journal of North African Studies*, vol. 19 no 5, 2014, pp. 733-750.

governing society, economy, and politics. They looked for inspiration to historical figures calling for the purging of alien influences from Islam, such as the eighteenth-century firebrand Muhammad ibn al-Wahhab. Wahhab was the antecedent of modern Salafism, a highly intolerant and strictly textualist understanding of Sunni Islam with an extremely narrow understanding of monotheism and a strong antipathy toward Christians, Jews, Sufi mystics and Shi'as. While originally marginal in the Muslim world, it grew to prominence thanks to the legitimacy Saudi Arabia derived from its custody of Islam's holiest sites, and the billions of petrodollars Saudi Arabia fed to Salafi movements across the globe.

Another wing of modern-day Islamism was founded in the first half of the twentieth century by ideologues like Hassan al-Banna, Abu A'la Mawdudi, and Sayyid Qutb. Banna, the founder of the Muslim Brotherhood, advocated the rejection of Western lifestyles and values, and urged a return to the purity of early Islam, as an all-encompassing system that governed everything from politics and economics to social questions. Banna's Brotherhood, the *Ikhwan-al Muslimeen*, aimed to liberate the whole Muslim world from foreign domination, and to establish a unified Islamic state. Mawdudi was Banna's South Asian equivalent, and is credited with redefining the concept of jihad, previously mainly seen as meaning defensive war, to legitimize a war that would enable Islam to take over the world. He argued that "Islam is a revolutionary ideology and programme which seeks to alter the social order of the whole world and rebuild it in conformity with its own tenets and ideals."[8] Qutb developed these ideas further, and concluded that present-day Muslim rulers were

8   Abul A'la Maududi, *Jihad in Islam*, Beirut: Holy Quran Publishing House, 1980, p. 5. (http://www.muhammadanism.org/Terrorism/jihah_in_islam/jihad_in_islam.pdf)

not really Muslims at all and could therefore be killed. In this way, Qutb paved the way for the various violent extremist groups in the Muslim world today that declare anyone who disagrees with them an unbeliever. As German author Matthias Küntzel details in a 2007 book, he also did more than anyone else to inject the notion of a Jewish world conspiracy into Islamist ideology.[9]

The Islamist ideology, then, is a thoroughly modern phenomenon. It is inspired by European totalitarian ideologies like communism and fascism, and like them is obsessed with political domination, rather than deliverance in the afterlife as traditional religion is. The rise of Islamism in the second half of the twentieth century, then, parallels the rise of totalitarian ideologies in Europe in the century's first half.

The Rise of Islamism

If the main powers of the Muslim world were decidedly secular in the middle of the twentieth century, that would change as Islamism began its rise to prominence in the 1970s.

Under Kemal Atatürk, Turkey broke firmly with its past by establishing a secular republic. The move included the abolition of both the Sultanate and the Caliphate that had prevailed in the Ottoman Empire. Turkey's constitution proclaimed the country a secular state, and replaced the Sharia with European legal codes imported wholesale and integrated into Turkish law. Atatürk adopted the Latin alphabet in place of the Arabic, banned religious orders and seminars, and prohibited the wearing of clerical

---

9   Matthias Küntzel, *Jihad and Jew-Hatred: Islamism, Nazism and the Roots of 9/11*, New York: Telos Press, 2007. See also Sayyid Qutb, *Past Trials and Present Tribulations: A Muslim Fundamentalist's View of the Jews*, Pergamon Press, 1987.

outfits. In the perhaps most symbolic move, the language of the call for prayer was changed from Arabic to Turkish.

Unlike communist countries, however, Kemalist Turkey never abolished or repressed religion per se. Nothing prevented Muslims from fulfilling the demands of their faith. The state, as the late President Süleyman Demirel told this author in 2007, only sought to ensure they could not force others to do as they did. Yet already in 1946, Turkey's leaders faced the advance of communism, and began to change their views on Islamic identity. Whereas it had previously been seen as an obstacle to modernity, it now appeared in a different light: as an antidote to Communism. The state therefore began to relax some of its most ardent secularist policies. By 1950, democratic elections led to the rise of the Democratic Party, which appealed to conservative voters that sought a lightening of restrictions on religion.

For the next forty years, Turkish politicians walked a tight balance between maintaining the secular state and simultaneously providing a greater role for religion. The 1980 military coup, in particular – which mainly targeted the Turkish left – sought to infuse religion into Turkish nationalism, in an attempt to counter the growth of leftist ideas. Subsequently, in the 1990s, the mainstream political parties lost legitimacy as a result of in-fighting, corruption and mismanagement, culminating in a severe financial crisis in 2000-2001. Meanwhile, Turkey's Islamist movement rose in influence, influenced mainly by the Naqshbandi-Khalidi tradition that emerged as the most well-organized Islamic community, and by Muslim Brotherhood thought that had begun to infiltrate Turkey from the 1950s onward. Islamist politics rose to the fore, coming to power first in a coalition government in 1996, and subsequently on its own when Recep Tayyip Erdogan's AKP won the 2002 election.

Iran followed a path that is in some respects both similar and different. Reza Shah Pahlavi, who had himself crowned in 1925, similarly sought to modernize and Europeanize Iran. As in Turkey, he sought to change the legal and educational system of the country as well as symbolic matters like dress. The shift in Iran was more gradual and piecemeal in the educational field, as the government only gradually took over schooling, and allowed the clergy to retain schools of its own, though the government managed to exert control over their curriculum. Similarly, the legal reforms in Iran were more gradual than in Turkey. The government at first set out to standardize Islamic law; then allowed religious courts to maintain authority over family matters. Sharia courts were only abolished and replaced with a European-modeled civil code in 1939, two years before Reza Shah was forced to abdicate.

But in Iran, symbolic measures were more aggressive than those in Turkey: the laws passed in the 1930s outlawed the wearing of the veil, and imposed western dress for both men and women. While Turkish laws also famously sought to change the way the population dressed, it never went as far as the Iranian campaigns to forcibly unveil the country's women. Iran's political instability also complicated matters: the abdication of Reza Shah allowed the clergy to make a comeback in the 1940s and 1950s. Then followed the more liberal regime of Mossadegh before its downfall in 1953, which led to a restoration of authoritarian monarchic rule. While the new king, Mohammad Reza Shah, continued to seek to modernize and westernize Iran, he failed as a result of several factors. One was the ostentatious opulence and arbitrariness of his rule, which differed from the more participatory civilian rule that prevailed in Turkey, although interspersed with short-lived military interventions. More importantly, because of the hierarchical nature of Shi'ism, Iran's government faced "a fairly institutionalized and financially independent clerical establishment outside the control of the state," which stands in sharp contrast to Turkey, where the state had taken control over the country's mosques and religious institutions through the Directorate of religious affairs. Iran never did, and as a result the religious communities became a center of resistance to the Shah, rather than as in Turkey, bodies that were largely under state control until the late 1980s.[10]

Across the Arab world, a secular nationalist ideology with socialist undertones became increasingly powerful in the middle of the twentieth century. While it was no unified movement, it rested on Arab nationalism as its main facet. While it was happy to accept Soviet money and support, Arab socialism was never Marxist in orientation, and never accepted the communist notion of class struggle. Its main proponent was the Baath party, which emerged in Syria in the 1940s, from where it spread also to Iraq and other Arab states. But it gained ground first in Egypt following the Free Officer's coup, which brought Gamal Abdul Nasser to power. While Nasser was not a Baathist, he shared the ideology of secular Arab nationalism coupled with socialist ideas. By the 1960s, Baathists came to power first in Syria and then in Iraq, and built authoritarian regimes that remained in power until 2003 in Iraq, and which continue to rule Syria to this day. While the regimes that emerged in Algeria and Libya sought to mix

---

10   Birol Baskan, "State Secularization and Religious Resurgence: Diverging Fates of Secularism in Turkey and Iran," *Politics and Religion*, vol. 27, 2014, pp. 28-50.

Islamic ideas with socialism, the Baath party remained secular. In Egypt, by contrast, secularism receded following Nasser's death. His successor, Anwar Sadat, loosened restrictions on the Muslim Brotherhood and other Islamist organizations in the wake of the 1967 defeat in the war against Israel. The 1971 constitution cited Sharia as "a source of legislation," which in 1980 was amended to read the "principal" source of legislation. From the 1980s onward, the secular regimes in the Arab world began to ossify and stagnate, both in ideological terms as well as in their ability to deliver public goods to their citizenry. Meanwhile, Islamist ideology was mounting its challenge to the established order.

The 1970s turned out to be critical in Islamism's rise to intellectual hegemony in the Muslim world. Islamist movements had begun to organize and gain traction. This pushed secular leaders on the defensive, and forced them to make concessions to Islamists. In Egypt, the Brotherhood and the even more radical Gama'a al-Islamiyya expanded their footprint, and Islamist extremists assassinated Anwar Sadat following his decision to make peace with Israel. In Pakistan, the secular Zulfiqar Ali Bhutto began bowing to Islamism: he declared Islam the state religion in 1973. Similarly, in Malaysia a rather liberal understanding of Islam gradually began to shift in a more radical direction in the 1970s. In Turkey, Necmettin Erbakan created the first legal Islamist political party in 1971, and throughout the decade that followed formed part of several coalition governments.

In all these cases, more secular or liberal elites chose to make concessions to Islamist sentiment in an effort to co-opt the Islamic movement and prevent more radical Islamists from gaining ground. In all cases, this strategy failed: concessions only whetted the appetite of Islamists for further Islamization.

The late 1970s were a turning point. The rise of Khomeini and the Iranian revolution was undoubtedly the first and most dramatic shift. Khomeini's unorthodox interpretation of Islamic government[11] broke with traditional Shi'a theology. But it showed that the creation of an Islamic state was not a pipe dream: it could happen in real life. This provided enormous inspiration to Islamist movements in the Sunni world: both the Muslim Brotherhood and the Turkish *Milli Görüs* movement developed a more pro-Iranian stance, something previously mitigated by widespread anti-Shi'a prejudice in the Sunni-majority countries.

Equally important in the long run was the siege of the Grand Mosque in Mecca by Salafi extremists, which proved critical to Saudi Arabia's exportation of Salafism. This event is vividly detailed in Yaroslav Trofimov's 2008 book on the topic.[12] In order to obtain the Ulama's approval for its repression of the siege, which involved military operations in this holiest of shrines , the Saudi monarchy was forced to accept many of the demands of the ultra-orthodox clergy. Not least, the monarchy essentially gave the clergy a free hand in spreading Salafi ideology across the globe.

The 1980 Turkish military coup purposefully opened the floodgates for the Islamization of society by ushering in the Turkish-Islamic synthesis, an idea that would form the background

---

11   Hamid Dabashi, *Theology of Discontent: The Ideological foundation of the Islamic Revolution in Iran*, London: Routledge, 2017; Nikki Keddie, *Iran and the Muslim: Revolution and Resistance*, New York: NYU Press, 1995.

12   Yaroslav Trofimov, *The Siege of Mecca: The 1979 Uprising at Islam's Holiest Shrine*, New York: Random House, 2008; Behlül Özkan, "The Cold-War Era Origins of Islamism in Turkey and Its Rise to Power," *Current Trends in Islamist Ideology*, November 2017.

for the meteoric rise of political Islam in Turkey in the 1980s and 1990s.[13] This notion was employed to shore up Turkish nationalism with greater Islamic content, in an effort to fend of the growing leftist mobilization among Turkey's urban youth. It led the Turkish state to begin sponsoring an Islamic revival, among other through greater Islamic content in education. With this followed a laxer attitude toward Islamist mobilization in society. Saudi-financed publishing houses emerged under the rule of a Turkish army that many viewed as a bastion of secularism. In fact, the military only turned against Islamism in the 1990s, when it feared it had lost control over the Islamist movement.

Finally, the rise of Zia ul-Haq in Pakistan following his military coup in 1978 formed the backdrop for the Islamization of that country, as he sought to implement full Sharia law. It was also a key step without which the international mobilization of *mujahideen* for the war in Afghanistan could not have happened. Indeed, the Afghan resistance to the Soviet occupation was initially relatively moderate and traditional. It was mainly because of Pakistan's insistence, with Saudi and American funding, that the bulk of the resources and fighters for the resistance were shifted in a radical Islamist direction.

Thus, by the late 1980s, Islamism had emerged as the dominant ideology across the Muslim world. This growing merger of religion and politics did not resolve any of the region's problems – but it created new ones, including lines of conflict between and among the main protagonists of the Greater Middle East.

---

13   Banu Eligür, *The Mobilization of Political Islam in Turkey*, New York: Cambridge University Press, 2010, pp. 85-135.

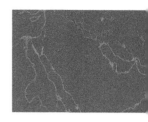

3.
GREATER MIDDLE EAST GEOPOLITICS AND THE COLD WAR

The middle of the twentieth century was the period of state formation in the Greater Middle East. During this time, the region's geopolitics were intimately woven into the global confrontations, from the second world war to the cold war. Only toward the late 1970s did the region begin to break out of the Cold War logic.

At the end of the First World War, the Ottoman Empire found itself on the losing side. Istanbul was occupied by British forces, French, Italian and Greek troops controlled various parts of the country. But the Turkish war of independence led by Kemal Atatürk re-established Turkish sovereignty over Anatolia. Atatürk renounced designs on former Ottoman holdings, with the exception of northern Syria and Iraq, which had initially been included in the territories claimed for the Turkish nation in the so-called National Pact of 1920. Atatürk's motto was "peace at home, peace in the world" – a vision that assumed Turkey would not encroach on other powers, but meanwhile jealously guard its own borders. In particular, Atatürk saw the former Middle Eastern possessions of the Empire only as a burden that Turkey should stay away from. He viewed them as backward provinces with unreliable populations, who had little to offer to a Turkey that should seek to develop at par with the most advanced countries of Europe. Indeed, with the exception of the 1974 invasion of Cyprus, Turkey remained true to this non-adventurist approach. That of course shifted with the rise of Recep Tayyip Erdogan to power, as will be seen later.

The foreign occupation on large parts of Turkey combined with Russian designs on the Turkish straits left a bitter aftertaste. Ever since, Turks have remained suspicious of foreign designs on Turkish territory. This created a paradox: a westernizing Turkey that was, simultaneously, highly suspicious of the intentions of its Western partners. As for relations with Russia, joint enmity against the British and French led Kemalist Turkey at first to enjoy good relations with Lenin's Russia. But it subsequently became clear that the Soviet authorities had the same designs on the Turkish straits as Czarist Russia had had, and that it now sought to export its Communist ideology. When the Second World War hit, Turkish authorities remained neutral, and initially leaned toward Britain and France in part because of fears of Soviet designs on the Turkish Straits and eastern Turkey – areas that had been the subject of bloody battles in the first world war.

This tilt remained the Turkish position as long as Hitler and Stalin were allied; Ankara reversed course only when Germany invaded the Soviet Union. While it remained neutral, from mid-1941 onward Turkey leaned increasingly in the direction of Germany, and only entered the war on the allied side in 1945, when Germany was defeated. Still, Turkey had maintained its independence during the war, an accomplishment in its own right.

Iran did not fare as well. From 1907 onward, the country had essentially been divided into a Russian sphere of influence in the north and a British one in the south. Still, Iranian king Reza Shah had sought to come out of this foreign domination by cultivating ties with Germany. This in turn triggered a preventive joint British and Soviet invasion of the country in the summer of 1941, prompted by the German invasion of Russia and fears that Hitler would occupy the oil fields of Baku, in present-day Azerbaijan, and then move south toward the Persian Gulf. While this dominance of foreign powers generated considerable resentment inside Iran, the monarchy was too weak to resist.

Further south, the British were at pains to rule over increasingly restive Arab lands. Egypt, under British control since 1882, was the scene of growing nationalist ferment. This forced London to grant Egypt independence in 1922, but Britain remained in charge of Egypt's defense, and continued to control Sudan to the south. Similarly, the British set up a loyal monarchy in Iraq in 1921, granted the territory independence in 1932, but maintained a military presence in the country. North Africa and the Middle East became a theater of the second world war as well, not least because Italy had forces in Libya that were reinforced by Nazi Germany. Concerns over German encroachments on British interests, as in Iran, led to a British invasion of Iraq (which had fallen under the influence of pan-Arabist factions) in May 1941. Egyptian territory was more directly involved in the war, as a battlefield between British forces and the German-Italian ones based in Libya. The British victory over Axis forces at El Alamein in 1942 is credited with playing an important role in turning the tide of the war, and setting up the Allied invasion of Italy in late 1943.

The Greater Middle East in the Cold War

The end of the war led to a rapid shift to the new conflict between the western allies and the Soviet Union. Iran and Turkey found themselves in a similar predicament: both faced increasingly hostile demands by the Soviet authorities. The Soviets made their designs on the Turkish straits clear, as control over these waterways would provide the Soviet navy with an outlet from the Black Sea to the world oceans. To the east, British forces withdrew from Iran in 1946, but Soviet forces stayed behind in violation of previous assurances. This crisis was one of the first of the emerging Cold War, as the Soviet Union sought to support the establishment of Kurdish and Azerbaijani states in northern Iran. It ended with a Soviet withdrawal from northern Iran following substantial U.S. pressure. Growing fear of Soviet intentions led both Turkey and Iran to side firmly with the West, and to intensify their security partnership with the United States. The Truman doctrine proved critical in providing assistance to Greece and Turkey, thus forestalling a Soviet move to secure control over the Balkans and the outlet to the Aegean. In Iran, the U.S. and UK backed up the Shah's rule by lending support to the Iranian forces that forced the downfall of the radical nationalist Mohammed Mosaddegh, who had nationalized the oil industry and whom the

U.S. and UK considered vulnerable to Soviet infiltration. While this intervention (or rather, the caricature of what had happened[14] became a *cause célèbre* for anti-Americanism, it helped sustain an American ally in power for several more decades. Until 1979, Iran and Turkey played a critical role in the U.S. policy of containment of the Soviet Union, and Turkey would continue to play this role until the end of the Cold War.

Meanwhile, the Arab world transitioned to greater independence, as a war-weary Britain was not in a position to preserve its pre-eminent role in countries like Egypt, Jordan and Iraq. France was similarly unable to preserve its influence in Syria and Lebanon. Instead the region now saw a growing confrontation between traditional monarchic rulers and more radical revolutionary movements inspired by socialist ideas. This dichotomy came to mirror the global east-west confrontation: the revolutionary forces sought Soviet assistance, while the traditional conservative rulers won support from the West. Already in the initial stages of World War Two, the U.S. had begun to appreciate the strategic importance of Saudi Arabia and its giant oil reserves. Toward the end of the war, the U.S. made sure to establish itself as the protector of the country, setting up a sometimes uneasy alliance that would remain in force for over half a century but be strained after the end of the Cold War by the Saudi support for global Islamism.

Yet another factor in the region was the formation of the State of Israel in 1948. Seen by many in the region as a Western project, it strengthened anti-western sentiment that revolutionary forces were able to capitalize upon. A coalition of Arab forces

---

14   Ray Takeyh, "The Coup Against Democracy that Wasn't," *Commentary*, December 2021.

invaded Israel immediately upon its creation, but this ended in the first of a series of humiliating failures by Arab powers to subdue the Jewish state. Then came to war of 1956, when former colonial powers France and Britan worked with Israel against Nasser's Egypt. This was followed by the wars of 1967 and 1973, all of which led to Israel victories.

The pro-British monarchy in Egypt did not last long: it was overthrown in 1952 by a military coup that led to the arrival to power of Gamal Abdel Nasser. Nasser's pan-Arabist ideas were the dominant ideological force in the region at the time, and spurred efforts to unite disparate Arab states. Nasser's rule and regional standing was strengthened by his nationalization of the Suez Canal, which prompted a British-French-Israeli military operation in 1957 that ultimately failed as a result of U.S. and Soviet opposition. In the aftermath, Egypt and Syria formed the United Arab Republic, a short-lived entity that dissolved when Syria left the construct in 1961. The UAR had prompted the monarchies in Iraq and Jordan to counter by announcing the creation of an Arab Federation. That idea, too, was stillborn as a military coup put an end to the Iraqi Kingdom in July 1958. The coup-plotters initially entertained the notion of joining the Syrian-Egyptian state, but eventually the conflicting ambitions of the three countries' leaders made such an arrangement impossible. Still, the Iraqi coup led the U.S. and UK to deploy forces to secure Jordan and Lebanon from further revolutionary change.

Meanwhile, Egypt turned increasingly toward the Soviet Union. Cairo had initially sought to play Washington and Moscow off against each other, but by the late 1950s thousands of Soviet advisors were deployed to Egypt. They played a key role in building the Egyptian military, even taking part in military operations against Israel. Iraq, meanwhile, slid ever more closely into the Soviet orbit following the 1958 coup. So did Syria after the advent of the Baath Party in 1966. The next year, South Yemen broke free from British rule, and became the only overtly Communist state in the Middle East. In sum, during the 1960s the influence of western powers declined visibly in the Arab world, with Soviet influence on the rise.

This Soviet rise was reversed in the 1970s, particularly as a result of Egypt's change of heart. Anwar Sadat, who succeeded Nasser, in 1972 sent home the Soviet troops – perhaps up to 20,000 – that had been stationed in the country, and moved Egypt closer to the United States and Saudi Arabia. This enabled the historic Camp David accords of 1978, which broke the universal Arab rejection of Israel's existence. Sadat was to pay with his life for this courageous act: he was assassinated three years later by Egyptian jihadists. Still, Egypt from then on was the cornerstone of U.S. policy in the Arab world, and one of the top recipients of American aid.

On the geopolitical level, a form of stalemate emerged. Two major Arab powers, Egypt and Saudi Arabia, aligned with the United States, while Syria and Iraq aligned against it. But the Cold War logic in the region was also weakened by Iraq's decision under Saddam Hussein to remove itself somewhat from the Soviet orbit, while its continued tensions with the other Baathist power, Syria, precluded the type of cordiality among the anti-Western group that existed between, for example, Saudi Arabia and Egypt.

The 1979 Iranian revolution broke the Cold War logic, as both the U.S. and Soviet Union supported Iraq in its war against

Iran. But in other respects, the Cold War logic simply moved east, into Afghanistan – where a Soviet invasion was opposed by an America-aligned coalition in which Riyadh and Islamabad played critical roles.

The U.S. and the Promotion of Islamism

In the Cold War context, the U.S. had a natural affinity with conservative forces in the region that sought to maintain a status quo, just as the Soviet Union found common language with revolutionary movements that sought to upset this status quo. Initially, this would have seemed uncontroversial: The U.S. supported conservative monarchies, as well as authoritarian anti-communist secular governments like those in Turkey and Iran. It is important to observe that the conservative monarchies rested on Islamic legitimacy, but not on Islamist ideology – they relied on Islamic conservative traditions, whereas the Islamist ideology that began to develop was itself revolutionary and radical rather than conservative and traditional. Of course, in Saudi Arabia and elsewhere, the Islamist ideology began infiltrating the mainstream with considerable implications.

But from an American perspective, Islamist forces appeared a tactical ally, or at least a lesser evil, compared to Soviet Communism. When regimes across the Sunni Muslim world began to stress their religious credentials and appeal to Islamists, there is no indication that the U.S. raised any objection. Quite to the contrary, there is considerable evidence that the U.S. tacitly or directly supported this development, seeing Islamic identity as the most effective antidote to leftist agitation that could benefit the Soviet Union.

This tendency is clearest in the case of Afghanistan, Pakistan and Turkey. In Afghanistan, Pakistani leaders preferred radical Islamist factions among the Afghan resistance to Soviet occupation. Aside from General Zia ul-Haq's ideological affinity with them, they were also less inclined to harbor territorial claims on Pakistan, compared to Pashtun nationalist groups that implicitly or explicitly laid claims on the country's North-West Frontier Province. They also proved to be more effective fighters. The United States willingly participated in the Pakistani and Saudi efforts to arm these groups, and can even be said to have played the role of the orchestra director.

In Pakistan itself, the U.S. relationship with Zia ul-Haq is equally telling. The 1971 loss of East Pakistan had exposed the weakness of the Pakistani national identity, and Pakistani leaders feared further ethnic secessionism in rump West Pakistan itself. Sindhis, Mohajirs and Pashtuns to varying extent resented the dominance of Punjabis in Pakistani politics and economy. The answer, Zia thought, was to emphasize the common Islamic identity among Pakistanis, along with enmity with India. The fact that the country's founder, Muhammad Ali Jinnah, had envisaged a state for Muslims that would be entirely secular was, at this time, a moot point.

The Islamization of Pakistan started before Zia's reign, but he took it further than many Pakistanis expected. He went as far as to introduce Islamic corporal punishment into the criminal justice system. Again, the U.S. saw this development in the light of the Cold War. Whatever qualms U.S. officials may have had about Zia's domestic policies, they appear to have seen them as a necessary evil to secure the unity of a crucial ally in the Cold War struggle.

The same logic applied in Turkey. Leftist activism had become widespread by the 1970s, and Turkish leaders appeared at a loss to contain it. The Turkish state mobilized right-wing nationalist mobs to counter the leftist agitation, but this resulted in chaotic street violence rather than anything resembling stability. Clearly, this was a threatening development in a NATO ally bordering the Soviet Union. By the late 1970s, street violence between leftists and nationalists was compounded by growing secessionist ambitions among Turkey's large Kurdish majority. As a result, Turkish center-right leaders came to support the idea, already mentioned, of a Turkish-Islamic synthesis. This line of thinking stressed the Islamic identity of Turkey, something that had the added benefit of appealing to religious conservative Kurds. Following the 1980 military coup, the military government enthusiastically promoted this new ideology. President Kenan Evren delivered speeches with the Koran in one hand, Islamic education being was expanded in schools, and 85,000 mosques were built in the 1980s. American policymakers appear to have endorsed this development as well. And why shouldn't they have? When pro-Soviet leftist activists protested a large U.S. naval visit to Istanbul in 1969, they were shouted down by the shock troops of the Islamist-nationalist National Turkish Student Association, the *Millî Türk Talebe Birliği*. This organization had a key slogan: "The only force that can destroy communism is Islam." As Halil Karaveli has described in his book *Why Turkey is Authoritarian*, this student organization is where Recep Tayyip Erdogan got his ideological formation.[15]

In Turkey as well as in Afghanistan and Pakistan, American

---

15   Halil Karaveli, *Why Turkey is Authoritarian*, London: Zed Books, 2018.

planners had little reason to oppose the rise of Islamism. This line of thinking was acknowledged by late Carter-era National Security Advisor Zbigniew Brzezinski, who was asked by a French journalist for the *Nouvel Observateur* in 1998 whether it had been a smart move to support Islamists that were to cause so much trouble. "What is more important in a world historical perspective," Brzezinski answered – "the Taliban or the fall of the Soviet Empire; a few frantic Muslims or the liberation of central Europe and the end of the Cold War?"[16] But in the years that followed, the Islamists that America had tacitly encouraged would, in search of a new enemy, turn on the United States itself.

The Post-Cold War Greater Middle East: The Collapse of Arab Powers and Weakening of American Hegemony

The final period in setting the current geopolitical scene took place in the period between the end of the Cold War and the 2011 Arab upheavals. Three key developments took place. First, several contenders for Arab leadership collapsed during this period. Second, Turkey and Iran advanced their ambitions for regional leadership. Finally, Islamism became a key driver of conflict.

As previously noted, a small group of Arab powers emerged to contend for power in the second half of the twentieth century. Saudi Arabia always laid claim to leadership on the basis of its custodianship of the holy sites, and backed this up with the financial resources brought by its oil wealth. Still, the Saudi kingdom was essentially defensive, and relied on U.S. support against perceived threats that included both Iran and another

---

16   *Le Nouvel Observateur*, 15-21 January 1998, p. 76.

contender for Arab leadership, Iraq. With a population larger than Saudi Arabia's, plentiful oil resources, and a radical regime under Saddam Hussein, Iraq prior to the 1990 Gulf War boasted of the world's fourth largest standing army. While it would prove an easy match for the U.S. military in Operation Desert Storm, Iraq inspired awe and fear among other Arab states.

Syria also laid claim to a leadership role, based on the Arab world's perhaps strongest relationship with Moscow, a similar investment in its military, and its own version of the Baathist ideology. Still, Syria's population is about half of Iraq's, and the country lacks abundant oil wealth, weakening its claim to leadership. Egypt, on the other hand, always stood out in the Arab world as a historic and intellectual center, and has by far the largest population of any Arab country – double the size of its closest contenders. It lacks oil wealth, however, and has thus continuously faced economic difficulties, particularly as the regime of Hosni Mubarak proved inept at reforming the Egyptian economy.

Over the past two decades, three of these powers have been turned from contenders for leadership to the scenes of proxy warfare between outside powers.

Iraq was the first to go. It was first reduced to size by the U.S. operation to restore Kuwait's independence following the Iraqi invasion of August 1990. While Iraq remained a force to be reckoned with, it was effectively thwarted by the two no-fly zones imposed by the United States in the country's north and south. Further, a *de facto* Kurdish state established itself in the north, and has been acting independently of Baghdad ever since. The 2003 U.S. invasion ended Saddam Hussein's regime, and the ensuing de-Baathification process put an end to the Iraqi state apparatus as it had been. Instead, Iraq turned into a weak state torn by sectarian strife, under U.S. suzerainty. Following the weakening and eventual departure of U.S. power, outside powers like Iran and Saudi Arabia have intervened in Iraq's internal affairs, Tehran in particular working hard to establish influence over Iraq through the use of allied political forces and Iranian-controlled armed militias.

Then, the Arab Upheavals reduced Egypt and Syria to size. The Egyptian revolution immediately led Egypt to be a scene of proxy confrontation rather than a leader in the Arab world. As we shall see, the Islamist government of Muhammad Morsi won support from Turkey and Qatar, while Saudi Arabia and the UAE strongly opposed it. Morsi's ouster less than two years later proved a major victory for the latter camp. Syria's regime survived, unlike those in Iraq or Egypt; but it did so at the price of international ostracism, enormous loss of life, and the Assad regime's acceptance of a subservient role to Iran.

The collapse in rapid succession of Iraq, Egypt and Syria is the perhaps most important factor in generating the current geopolitical rivalry in the Greater Middle East. It allowed two new developments: the rise to prominence of Gulf monarchies, and the expanded role of non-Arab powers like Turkey and Iran. Saudi Arabia was always a contender for leadership, and remained, so to speak, the last man standing among the traditional contenders. In recent years, it has been joined by small states like the UAE and Qatar that have played outsize roles in regional geopolitics – something that would not have been possible without the collapse of major Arab powers.

The vacuum created was not just filled by small Arab

powers. In fact, as will be seen in the next several chapters, this process provided opportunities for Turkey and Iran to intervene in regional geopolitics. This was nothing new as far as Iran was concerned, as the Islamic republic had harbored such ambitions since its inception. The extent of Tehran's gambit, however, was new. Turkey's entry into the fray, by contrast, was a new development. Ankara's foreign policy orientation had been toward the West since the 1920s, and Turkey had been a relatively minor player in the Middle East until the 1990s. But it would gradually take on a greater role, first by building an alignment with Israel under secularist rule in the 1990s. A decade later, the Islamist government under Erdogan would make a 180-degree turn, and instead base Turkey's claim to leadership on its championing of the Muslim Brotherhood's Islamist ideology across the region. The rise of nationalist bureaucrats after 2016 is changing the nature of Turkey's role again.

This point concerning the role of ideology is key to our understanding of regional geopolitics. While the emerging rivalries to some degree stem from traditional "realpolitik" struggles for power and influence, they have also been informed by the key players' stance toward Islamist mobilization. These stances have changed considerably in the past two decades.

As the next chapter will show, Tehran has continued to support Shi'a mobilization, and capitalized on non-Sunni communities' fears of Sunni radicalism, as tools to secure regional pre-eminence. But that merely an acceleration of Iran's approach, which has been consistent since 1979. The Saudi and Turkish approaches, however, have shifted dramatically by comparison. Saudi Arabia went from being the chief sponsor of

Islamic radicalism worldwide, to seeing Islamist mobilization as a threat to regional stability and to its own survival. This process began with Saudi Arabia's reaction to Al Qaeda's rise, continued with the Arab Upheavals, and accelerated with the rise to power of Crown Prince Muhammad bin Salman.

By contrast, under Erdogan Turkey went from being largely a status quo power to become the key supporter of the Muslim Brotherhood and aligned forces across the region, while seeking to use Sunni Islamist mobilization to build a "sphere of influence" in the Middle East and North Africa.

These diverging perceptions of political Islam are key to understanding regional geopolitics. The Saudi-Iranian rivalry has long been colored by the hostility between Wahhabi and Shi'a manifestations of Islam. But Turkey's turn to Islamism for some time led it to be closer to Iran, while putting it in direct confrontation with Saudi Arabia and its allies. This may appear quite bewildering: the Saudis once implored upon Egyptian rulers to treat the Muslim Brotherhood more kindly, whereas more recently Turkish support for that organization was a key reason for the growing hostility between Riyadh and Ankara. In recent years, as will be seen, Turkey's turn in a nationalist direction removed some of the tension in relations with Saudi Arabia while putting Ankara at collision course with Tehran.

Underlying all these rivalries is the waning role of the United States in Middle East geopolitics. The United States featured prominently in the calculations of regional powers, not least because certain American policies were once bipartisan in nature and thus predictable. This was the case for the U.S. policy of dual containment of Iran and Iraq; and its staunch support for both Saudi Arabia and Turkey. But in the past decade, U.S. policy has been all but predictable, and become increasingly partisan in nature. To some extent, this began with the Bush Administration's decision to invade Iraq, a move that was highly controversial both at home and abroad, and which was found to rest on shaky foundations. Still, Bush's handling of Iraq was an issue of policy instruments rather than the fundamental approach to regional geopolitics. From this perspective, it was the Obama Administration that engaged in a rethink of U.S. policy, proposing to reach out to Iran. This initiative was bold, and was informed by an urge to disentangle America from the geopolitics of the Greater Middle East. If a *modus vivendi* could be found with Iran, the U.S. would be able to cease functioning as the protector of the Gulf States, and a balance of power could develop in the region that might no longer require U.S. intervention. Of course, the Trump Administration went back to a traditional policy of hostility to the Islamic Republic, whereas Joe Biden's election led to the return of the Obama-era approach. All in all, this means that regional leaders can no longer count on long-term U.S. policies, as these are no longer predictable and shift according to the whims of U.S. electoral cycles.

This lack of clarity has forced regional powers to rely increasingly on their own devices, and to conclude their own regional alignments to further their interests. The most obvious example of this is the emerging alignment between Israel and the Gulf States. But U.S. vacillation has also invited the intervention of other outside powers – with Russia's re-entry into the region being the most dramatic manifestation of this trend, with China following closely behind.

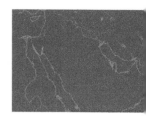

4.
IRAN, THE PRIME MOVER

Iran is the prime mover in Greater Middle Eastern geopolitics. By its size and location, Iran is the most consequential of regional powers. But more than that, the revolutionary agenda of the Islamic Republic has set in motion processes that, generally speaking, other regional actors have been responding to. Iran's shift from a status quo power to an actively revisionist one has been, for four decades, what others have had to relate to.

Iran's Centrality and Vulnerability

Iran lies at the center of Greater Middle Eastern geopolitics. The sheer size of the country, at over 600,000 square miles, makes it twice the size of Turkey. Its location further strengthens its centrality: it connects the Persian Gulf with Central Asia, and the Indian subcontinent with the Middle East. But this centrality also implies an exposure to outside challenges, especially at times when Iran has had weak central government. Historically, the country has alternated between periods of strong, expansionist government – think the Safavid dynasty in the sixteenth century – and weak, fragmented authority, as was the case in much of the eighteenth and nineteenth centuries.

This explains why Iran was drawn into the geopolitical competition between Great Britain and Russia in the nineteenth century. During the British Raj, only a little over a hundred thousand Britons controlled India, whose population was over 200 million. This is one reason the British were so fearful of another European power usurping its rule over the subcontinent. As the nineteenth century progressed, Russia began expanding its control over Central Asia. This led to famed "Great Game" or "Tournament of Shadows" between Britain and Russia, which centered on British fears of an impending Russian invasion of British India. When Russia pressed south in wars against Iran in 1812-13 and then 1828-29, it grabbed territory from Iran that presently forms the states of the South Caucasus, and increased its intervention in Iranian internal affairs. Conversely, the British expanded their relations with Iran's Qajar dynasty in order to bolster Iran as a buffer state protecting British India from a Russian invasion.

This "Great Game" officially ended in 1907 with a formal Anglo-Russian convention that divided Iran into spheres of influence. Britain recognized Russian interests in large parts of northern Iran, and Russia recognized British interests in southeastern Iran. After the Bolshevik revolution, Britain became the pre-eminent power in Iran, and following the discovery of large oil reserves, the British government – through the Anglo-Persian Oil Company (the precursor to British Petroleum) – asserted control over Iran's oil. Immediately following the German invasion of the Soviet Union in 1941, London and Moscow again agreed to assert control over Iran – this time to stop a potential Nazi invasion, which they feared would follow the ongoing German effort to invade the oil-rich Russian Caucasus and take Baku. Not staying at that, the British in September 1941 forced the abdication of Iranian monarch Reza Shah, whom they suspected of German sympathies, to be replaced with his more pro-British son, Muhammad Reza Pahlavi.

This European domination of Iran did not end with the second world war – the Soviet Union sought to remain in Iran after the end of the war, but was forced to retreat by the allied powers. British influence over Iran's oil industry continued until the populist Iranian government of Muhammad Mossadegh sought to nationalize the industry in 1951. The downfall of Mossadegh in 1953 led to a new arrangement that brought the famed American oil companies known as the "Seven Sisters" into prominence alongside BP.

All in all, Iran's tumultuous history during the nineteenth and early twentieth century led to widespread resentment against European powers, and their interventions into Iranian affairs heightened the already prevalent conspiracism in the country about the evil designs of European powers upon Iran.

Meanwhile, Muhammad Reza Shah sought to develop and strengthen Iran while remaining a key ally of the West. He embarked on a major effort to industrialize the country, while aggressively seeking to secularize Iranian society, which he saw as held back by religious backwardness. His economic reforms led to the development of domestic industries focused on automotive and home appliance sectors, among other, while he countered feudal interests by championing land reform. He also developed a nationalist agenda, and while his support for the coup against

Mossadegh is widely remembered, his ability to wrest control of Iran's oil from the multinational companies in the 1970s is less so. In other words, he was able to nationalize the country's most valuable asset and take the lead among oil producing nations in hiking the price of oil multiple times – all while maintaining his close alignment with the United States. But he also used Persian language and ethnic, Persian-based nationalism as the identity of the state, to the detriment of the ethnic minorities, including Turks and Arabs. This stood in sharp contrast to Iran's past as a multi-ethnic state that had frequently been ruled by Turkic dynasties.

His social reforms were more controversial inside Iran, however. He championed the liberation of women, and abolished requirements that elected officials or judges had to be Muslim and male. This attracted the wrath of the religious establishment. And as we have seen, unlike in neighboring Turkey, the religious establishment was strongly institutionalized, and maintained significant influence over the country's education system. The Shah's efforts at secularization were therefore at once more shallow than those in Turkey, as well as more aggressive. On one hand, the efforts to unveil women were more forceful in Iran than in Turkey, but on the other the monarchy had never been able to suppress organized clerical opposition nor put religious affairs under state control. This – and the Shah's profligate spending on palaces and private consumption – provided permissive conditions for the emergence of a radical challenger from among the clergy, in the shape of Ruhollah Khomeini.

Revolutionary ideology

In Shi'a Islam, politically "quietist" traditions had traditionally been dominant. In Shi'a theology, the notion of the *Mahdi* – the hidden imam – is central. Twelver Shi'ism, the majority branch prevalent in Iran, holds that the twelfth imam went into "occultation" in the late ninth century, and will return to rule the world in end times. In waiting for the hidden imam, the traditionally dominant view among the Shi'a had been that there can be no perfect government run by humans, and that Muslims should generally obey a rightful ruler, while waiting for the return of the *Mahdi*. Shi'a clergy had occasionally dared to counsel the ruler to follow the principles of Islam. But nowhere in this tradition is there a notion of clerics themselves assuming the reins of the state.

Ruhollah Khomeini would change that. Born in central Iran around 1900, Khomeini rose in the ranks of the Iranian clergy and distinguished himself as an opponent of the secularizing policies of the Shah. He gained recognition as a Grand Ayatollah in the early 1960s, and made his mark as a leading opponent of the Shah's modernizing reforms launched in 1963. His fervent attacks on the Shah landed him in prison on several occasions before he was forced into exile. He spent most of this exile in the Shi'a holy city of Najaf in Iraq, before moving to France in 1978.

Khomeini's political thought was clearly modern and radical rather than ultra-conservative. In his past, he had been known to study philosophy – including that of Plato and Aristotle – and was thus open to non-Islamic influences on his political philosophy. He also integrated leftist, populist ideas centering on the dichotomy between oppressors and oppressed into his ideology. He was also clearly influenced by radical Islamist thinkers in the

Sunni world, not least Egyptian Muslim Brotherhood firebrand Sayyid Qutb.

Khomeini's virulent anti-Semitism was, just as in Qutb's case, central to his ideology. This is remarkable as it is quite alien to the Iranian scene, where such hatred of Jews had never been widespread. Khomeini had been exposed to the Nazi propaganda of an alleged Jewish world conspiracy, which was spread across Iran by Germany's Radio Zeesen in the 1930s. It was further strengthened by Qutb's obsession with the Jews. German scholar Matthias Küntzel has described these connections in detail – establishing that there is a clear Nazi origin to the transformation of traditional prejudice against Jews in the Muslim world to the genocidal hatred that lies at the heart of the modern Islamist ideology.[17] More broadly, conspiracism was central to Khomeini's worldview – he tended to see every individual disagreeing with his ideology as an "agent" of the Jews or Americans (whom he, of course, saw as controlled by the Jews). First and foremost among the targets of his hatred was of course the Shah, whom he labeled a servant of the Jews.

Khomeini's political ideology was truly revolutionary. In place of the traditional quietism of Shi'a Islam, he proposed a completely new theory: that of the rule of the supreme Islamic jurist, *Vilayat-e-Faqih*. In the traditional approach, Shi'a theology had recognized the legitimacy of a monarchy, with Islamic jurists remaining focused on Islamic jurisprudence. Khomeini, by contrast, declared that Islam considers monarchy inherently illegitimate, as it cannot provide for the consistent application of Islamic law. Instead, while waiting for the return of the twelfth

17   Matthias Küntzel, *Germany and Iran: From the Aryan Axis to the Nuclear Threshold*, transl. Colin Meade, Candor, NY: Telos Press, 2015.

imam, political power should belong to the clergy itself, and particularly the most exalted religious leader. Incidentally, that would have been Khomeini himself.

Just how alien Khomeini's thought was to traditional Shi'a thinking is best illustrated by the fact that only one among the dozen or so living Grand Ayatollahs at the time supported Khomeini's ideas. The perhaps most important cleric of the time, Ayatollah Mohammed Kazem Shariatmadari, outright rejected Khomeini's doctrine, something that led to his character assassination and landed him in house arrest until his death in 1986. the only Grand Ayatollah that supported Khomeini, Hossein Ali Montazeri, eventually disavowed Khomeinism entirely in 1988, when Khomeini decreed that Sharia itself – contrary to his earlier teachings – was subjugated to the primacy of the Islamic state, loyalty to which he claimed surpassed all other obligations in Islam.

Khomeini was not content with power in Iran: his ideology was made for export, and from the outset he made clear he aimed for power across the region. He expected the form of government he launched in Iran to spread across the Muslim world and beyond. Just as his Sunni counterparts in the Muslim Brotherhood and its more extreme offshoots, Khomeini had designs that were truly global. In 1979, he expressed his objective succinctly: "Until the cry 'there is no god but Allah' resounds over the whole world, there will be struggle." By this he specifically meant the establishment of an Islamic state across the globe – with his own system of government replacing both capitalism and communism, which he equally condemned.

Khomeini may have been an outlier and perhaps a power-hungry paranoid, but he was also immensely charismatic and a brilliant strategist. While becoming the leader of the opposition to the Shah in exile, he somehow managed to be everything to everyone – convincing both Iranian leftists and Western observers that he was just a pious spiritual leader who had no ambition to rule the country but only to usher in a progressive and democratic government. But as historian Bernard Lewis pointed out then and subsequently, Khomeini's true nature was obvious from a reading of his treatise on Islamic Government, published in Persian and Arabic, which Lewis had checked out of the Princeton University Library. This treatise, a collection of lectures given during his exile in Iraq, spelled out in great detail the system of *vilayat-e-faqih* and Khomeini's authoritarian and extremist ideology.

Khomeini's success, his charisma and his novel and radical Islamist ideology raised the prospect of his thinking being embraced first by the region's Shi'a, and perhaps, Sunnis as well. As will be seen in subsequent chapters, Khomeini's success in actually establishing Islamic government led to profound repercussions in the Sunni world. Islamist groups there began to reassess their traditional disdain for the heretic Shi'a, and instead came to see Iran as an example to be emulated. Turkish Islamists certainly did so, as did the Muslim Brotherhood, understandably so since Khomeini's ideology was so close to theirs, and inspired by the Brotherhood's own ideologues. It is no exaggeration to say that Khomeini's rise prompted other powers to embark on their own efforts to instrumentalize religion for their own purposes. This happened most gravely with the Saudi kingdom's decision to embrace Salafi ideology, but also with the Turkish generals' promotion of the "Turkish-Islamic synthesis" following the 1980 coup. In this sense, Iran has truly been a prime mover in Middle East geopolitics as well as in ideological development.

Power in the Islamic Republic

Khomeini remained in power with unquestioned authority until his death in 1989. His opportunistic approach was visible to the end, when he reversed himself on a very central issue: the qualifications of the *vali-e-faqih*, or supreme leader. A decade earlier, he had insisted that only the most exalted among Islamic jurists (such as he styled himself) could serve as supreme leader, but in 1989 he faced the reality that the most exalted Shi'a clerics did not even support his very theory of government. So, he reversed course, in order to be able to anoint a rather junior cleric – Ali Khamenei – who was not even a full Ayatollah at the time. But Khamenei had the advantage of being fully committed to Khomeini's ideology – he had translated the works of Sayyid Qutb into Persian decades earlier, indicating his ideological commonality with Khomeini.

After Khomeini's death, the supreme leader could no longer govern with the same charismatic authority as Khomeini had. Instead, a somewhat more pluralistic system emerged, though one where the supreme leader maintained final authority. Still, the Iranian system features pseudo-democratic aspects – the parliament and president are elected by direct ballot, although the candidates must be vetted and approved by a "guardian's council" of religious clerics loyal to the supreme leader.

This has nevertheless allowed for a modicum of political

participation and for the regime to allow the public mood to let off steam. Thus, the presidency has seen more moderate, conciliatory figures elected such as Mohammad Khatami in the 1990s and Hassan Rouhani in the 2010s. It has also seen hardliners like Mahmoud Ahmadinejad in the 2000s and Ibrahim Raisi in the 2020s. Like in any authoritarian regime, there is factionalism in Iran, and disagreement on how to approach the world – even on how to deal with the United States. But time and time again, it has been clear that elected leaders are essentially powerless against the ideological centers of power. As recently as in April 2021, a tape was leaked in which Iranian foreign minister Javad Zarif complained loudly of the interference of the Iranian Revolutionary Guards Corps (IRGC), adding that he had "zero influence" over Iranian foreign policy. In the past, former Presidents Akbar Hashemi Rafsanjani and Hassan Rouhani had made similar comments. Indeed, The IRGC has over time grown into a state within a state, exercising enormous influence over Iran's politics, economy and foreign policy.

State within a State: the IRGC and Quds Force

One of the first steps Khomeini took after the revolution was to consolidate a military force loyal to himself and committed to his revolutionary ideology. To do so, he formally merged the different existing Islamist militias into the Iranian Revolutionary Guard Corps. This force had several objectives, first among which was to safeguard the revolution from internal challenges – not least the Iranian army, where support for the revolution was unclear and where sympathies for the monarchy remained strong. Officially, the IRGC early on defined as its main objective to maintain the *vilayat-e-faqih* system of government and to promote jihad. Importantly, its leaders have repeatedly made the point that the word "Iran" is nowhere in its title, indicating the broader ambitions of the IRGC.

The IRGC also incorporated a volunteer force known as the *Basij*, consisting largely of youth drawn from loyal constituencies in conservative and lower-income areas. This force has been used to police the population's adherence to Islamic dress and behavior codes, while on many occasions it has been deployed to crack heads of opponents to the regime, most visibly during the 2009 "Green revolution."

Domestically, the IRGC has grown in power inside Iran. In the 1980s, Khomeini relied on the IRGC to purge the fellow travelers of the revolution. This included the communist Tudeh party, the leftist-Islamist Mojahedin-e-Khalq organization, and non-Islamist political leaders that had held key roles in the transitional government after the revolution. This meant that after Khomeini's death, the IRGC had enormous leverage over other centers of power. It used this leverage in particular during the presidency of the moderate and reform-minded President Khatami in the late 1990s, when the IRGC Head repeatedly warned publicly of the dangers of weakening the core principles of the revolution, threatened to overthrow Khatami, and acted to suppress student protests.

The continuous rise of pro-reform and anti-regime sentiment in Iran, visible from the late 1990s onwards, also led to a realignment of forces. Whereas Supreme Leader Khamenei at first sought to balance the power of the IRGC, over time he came to see the IRGC as the praetorian guard that was absolutely necessary to safeguard the revolution (and his own position) against the growing portions of the population that seemed to desire otherwise.

This was also the time when the IRGC began gobbling up large parts of the Iranian economy. As a concession to the IRGC, political leaders had given IRGC-affiliated business groups preferential treatment in the reconstruction projects following the war against Iraq. The IRGC then got involved in a variety of sectors of the economy, ranging from agriculture to banking. Its economic clout grew immensely during the presidency of Mahmoud Ahamdinejad in the early 2000s. Ahmadinejad, a former member of the *basij*, formed a cabinet where former IRGC officers held key positions, and opened the floodgates for the further expansion of the IRGC's economic empire. Suffice it to note that in 2009, IRGC businesses paid $8 billion to take control of 50% of the dominant actor in the Iranian telecom industry, the Telecommunications Company of Iran. Under the Presidency of Ibrahim Raisi since 2021, the IRGC has further strengthened its positions. Raisi appointed a former IRGC commander Vice President for economic affairs, several IRGC officers hold ministerial positions, and IRGC officers feature prominently among officials appointed governors in Iran's provinces. Author Nader Uskowi estimates that up to half the Iranian economy is in the hands of the IRGC, and analyst Ali Alfoneh has launched the theory that the rise of the IRGC threatens changing the nature of the Iranian regime to a military dictatorship, particularly after the demise of Khamenei.[18]

---

18   Nader Uskowi, *Temperature Rising: Iran's Revolutionary Guards and Wars in the Middle East*, Lanham, MD: Rowman& Littlefield, 2019. Ali Alfoneh, *Iran Unveiled: How the Revolutionary Guards is Turning Theocracy into Military Dictatorship*, Washington DC: AEI Press, 2013.

This economic power helped strengthen the IRGC's independence. Because it controls its own sources of income, it is not entirely dependent on budgetary support for its activities – further strengthening its leverage in relation to the civilian elements of the Iranian political system.

The IRGC, furthermore, was never intended to solely focus on domestic affairs. In line with the intention to export the revolution, the IRGC has been involved in a variety of operations outside the country's borders. Originally a special intelligence department was created during the Iran-Iraq war, which eventually was turned into an independent service branch in 1988. This was the now-famous "Quds Force," symbolically named after the Arabic term for Jerusalem, and officially designed to "liberate" Muslim lands.

In practice, the Quds Force became a key vehicle for the expansion of Iranian influence and terror. U.S. General Stanley McChrystal described the organization as analogous to a combination of the CIA and the Joint Special Operations Command. Under the legendary commander Major General Qassem Soleimani, who led the Quds Force from 1998 to his death at the hands of an American missile in January 2020, the Quds Force grew to be a major force in Middle Eastern affairs and beyond – and Soleimani himself gained prominence as perhaps the second-most influential individual in Iran. Analysts have concluded that the Quds Force is accountable only Supreme Leader Khamenei, and operates in a manner entirely uncoordinated with the Iranian Ministry of Foreign Affairs or other civilian bodies.

The Quds Force was active in Afghanistan in the late 1990, sent in to bolster the Northern Alliance forces opposing the Taliban –

a grouping that Iran at first considered an extension of its rivals Saudi Arabia and Pakistan. Following the U.S. invasion of Iraq, the Quds Force played a critical role in countering America's presence in Iraq. It assembled and coordinated as well as trained and armed Iraqi Shi'a militias, and provided the improvised explosive devices to the militias that killed or injured hundreds of American servicemen. The Quds Force is also suspected of being Tehran's interlocutor with Al Qaeda. As will be seen in a later chapter, it has played a critical role in implementing Iran's "arc of resistance," Iran's efforts to undermine states from Lebanon in the west to Yemen in the east.

Iran's Regional Role

Iran's transformation from a status quo power under the Shah to a revolutionary regime affected the calculus of every other power, making Iran the prime mover to which everyone else was reacting. This has continued to be the case for four decades, and to some extent increasingly so as Iran has benefited from the decline of regional powers like Iraq and Syria, and used unconventional warfare to establish itself as the manager of the instability that has ensued. Saudi Arabia and Turkey both reacted with shock to Iran's transformation – both launching their own ideological response to Khomeini. The Saudis, as we shall see, began to spread extremist Salafi ideology across the region and beyond, while Turkey's military junta promoted the notion of a "Turkish-Islamic" synthesis. In both cases, other factors contributed to the decision to do so, but it is not likely this would have happened in the absence of the ideological challenge launched by Khomeini.

At the same time, while the Iranian regime is a dangerous and expansionist one, it is also internally weakened. Among the three large powers, it is perhaps the weakest internally – with large swathes of the Iranian population being virulently opposed to the regime. Protest in Iran has mounted in the past decade to an extent that has led to growing speculation about the impending collapse of the regime; but thus far, such hopes have come to naught. The rise of the IRGC is perhaps the main reason for this, as it has established itself as the guarantor of the regime with a proven willingness to shed large amounts of Iranian blood to stay in power.

5.
SAUDI ARABIA AND THE GULF MONARCHIES

The decline of the traditional Arab powers led to the emergence of the Gulf monarchies as key players in the Sunni Arab world. These monarchies, led by Saudi Arabia, have over the years combined religious authority and oil-generated financial clout to exert influence not just in the Arab world but globally. The descent of Iraq, Syria and Egypt into turmoil explains how Saudi Arabia emerged as the leader of the conservative Sunni faction, and even more, how diminutive states like the UAE and Qatar have been able to be major brokers in Middle Eastern regional politics.

The threat emanating from Iran has been the key factor bringing these monarchies together, and animating their response to regional events. The common fear of Iran has led them to seek external support from the United States; but given the twists and turns of U.S. policy on Iran, Saudi Arabia and its neighbors have been forced to hedge. Internal shifts have also played an important role. Saudi Arabia, and to a lesser extent other Gulf monarchies, hold a large part of the responsibility for the global spread of Salafi-Jihadi and more generally Islamist ideas. But in recent years, their approach to Salafi zealots has changed. The UAE was the first to express its skepticism toward political Islam and the Muslim Brotherhood specifically. More recently, Saudi Arabia followed suit – first by opposing the Brotherhood, and subsequently by ending the informal pact the ruling Saudi monarchy had with its own Salafi clergy – with the Kingdom going so far as to officially support the notion of "moderate Islam."

Arab Rivalries and Saudi Arabia's Rise

The end of the first world war augmented the role of Western powers in the Arab world. Britain and France were the key drivers in the division of the Middle Eastern domains of the Ottoman Empire, and helped delineate the boundaries of the Middle East as early as 1916, when the two signed the Sykes-Picot agreement. This led to the establishment of the modern states of Iraq, Lebanon and Syria as well as the Palestine mandate. Only one Arab state, Saudi Arabia, was never ruled by Western powers. The Saudi kingdom emerged in its third iteration in the early years of the twentieth century, expanding to its present borders by the late 1920s.

It was after the Second World War that the modern geopolitics of the Middle East began to take form. The overextended British and French were unable to maintain their colonial realm. In spite of French resistance, Syria became an independent republic by 1946, and Britain granted independence to Jordan the same year. The British had already granted *formal* independence to Egypt and Iraq, while attempting to treat the two as protectorates. In both cases, the British presence was brought to an end by military uprisings: the Free Officer's coup of 1952 abolished the Egyptian Monarchy and evicted the British, and similarly the 1958 coup ended the short-lived Hashemite monarchy in Iraq, replaced with a left-leaning republic. By the late 1960s, both Iraq and Syria were under the control of separate wings of the Arab nationalist Baath party.

The contours of the region's geopolitics were formed in great part by the cold war. The Arab states newly liberated from Western colonial rule – Egypt, Iraq and Syria – were now Republics that paid allegiance to Arab nationalism and to a socialist ideology. Aside from Morocco in the far West of the Arab world, only in Jordan did the monarchy survive, a testament to the political acumen of King Hussein, who reigned from 1952 to his death in 1999. The three radical Arab states emerged as the most powerful military powers of the Arab World. They also had the most significant populations: in 1960, Egypt had 27 million people, Iraq seven million and Syria five million. By comparison, Saudi Arabia had only four million, and Jordan barely a million. The Arab Gulf states, still British protectorates, numbered only in the tens or low hundreds of thousands.

Given the recent and often artificial nature of their statehood, Arab states tended to have weak internal legitimacy. With the partial exception of Egypt, few of them commanded any allegiance to a national idea, as cross-cutting allegiances to tribes and religious sects undermined the novel concept of nation-states. Further, the Pan-Arab nationalist ideology of the rulers often undermined their own nation-building process. Egypt and

Syria even formed a short-lived United Arab Republic in 1958, lasting only three years – but it managed to spook the Hashemite rulers of Jordan and Iraq sufficiently to form a United Hashemite Federation uniting the realms of two cousins who ruled these countries. It proved even more short-lived than the UAR, however, as the Iraqi revolution brought an end to the project only five months later. The new Iraqi leaders considered joining the UAR, but eventually decided against it. Iran laid claim to Bahrain, Iraq laid claim to Kuwait, among myriad other territorial squabbles the region's states have had over recent decades.

As the largest Arab country, Egypt played a predominant role in Middle Eastern geopolitics. Under Gamal Abdel Nasser, who led the 1952 coup, Egypt effectively helped the Soviet Union nullify the U.S. and British ambition to build a coalition of states from Turkey to Pakistan that sought to thwart Soviet advances into the region. The U.S.-led coalition was known first as the Baghdad Pact, and following Iraq's exit from the organization in 1958, as the Central treaty Organization (CENTO). It then included only non-Arab states – Turkey, Iran and Pakistan along with the UK. The Soviets essentially leapfrogged CENTO by establishing close ties with radical Arab states at the heart of the Middle East.

Saudi Arabia emerged as an important player in regional geopolitics as a result of several factors. It derived a significant appeal as a result of its religious importance as the custodian of the holiest places of Islam, strengthened by the fact that it had not been colonized. Its rulers were also vehemently anti-Communist. Furthermore, with the rapid increase in oil revenues in the 1970s, Saudi Arabia became excessively wealthy, and was thus able to develop an outsize influence across the Arab world, as well as build a strong military force.

During the second world war, the United States identified the stability and security of Saudi Arabia as a crucial national interest, a result primarily of the country's gigantic oil reserves. As British influence in the region waned, the U.S. came to build its regional strategy on three key Middle Eastern states: Israel, Iran and Saudi Arabia. This was a delicate dance, not least because of the controversial nature of American support for Israel. Saudi rulers, always pragmatic, consistently sided with the Arab states on the Israel issue, although they did not seem overly excited about the Palestinian cause. It was a policy designed mainly to ensure domestic stability, given the influence of Wahhabi thought in Saudi society, and out of fear that Saudi rulers would be targeted by Egyptian, Syrian and Iraqi leaders as insufficiently committed to the Arab cause.

For its part, the Saudi monarchy was acutely aware of its vulnerability to external attack, given its large territory, attractive oil fields, and population of only a few million. Still, the relationship with the U.S. was not uncontroversial, not least because of the ultra-Orthodox views of the influential Salafi clergy, to whom dependence on a Christian power was abhorrent. This made American military presence on Saudi soil another touchy issue in the bilateral relationship.

What really mattered to Saudi rulers was not the situation in the Levant, but the competition for dominance in the Gulf. This is where Saudi Arabia was highly vulnerable, not least because its oil wealth was located in the country's eastern provinces, close to the Gulf itself and within striking distance of Iraq and Iran. The

UK's military presence in the smaller emirates of the Gulf served as a stabilizing force until the end of the 1960s, and London faced no real demand for independence. But under the Labor party's rule and facing economic difficulties at home, the UK announced in 1968 it would withdraw from the Gulf militarily. The U.S., bogged down in the Vietnam conflict, was not yet in a position to fill the vacuum. In 1971, seven Emirates from what had been known as the "Trucial States" joined forces to form the United Arab Emirates under the leadership of oil-rich Abu Dhabi. Qatar and Bahrain elected not to join the union and became independent states. Oman was already nominally independent, and Kuwait had gained statehood in 1961.

The British departure kindled a number of territorial disputes over islands in the Persian Gulf as well as over border demarcation. But overall, the Gulf region remained relatively stable. The relations between the three main powers – Saudi Arabia, Iran and Iraq – were never amicable, but the brief conflict between Iran and Iraq in the mid-1970s was the main controversy of the decade. Meanwhile, the region's powers had a common interest in taking control over oil pricing from Western companies, and pushing up the price of oil. The opportunity to do this came with the 1973 Arab-Israeli war, which provided the oil-producing states with an excuse to hike prices. This became possible as a result of a rapid shift in the power relations between producer states and multinational oil companies, in which the governments succeeded in getting the upper hand over companies that had long dictated conditions and prices over regional governments.

It was in the 1970s that the Gulf monarchies and particularly Saudi Arabia became the financial powerhouses that they are today. The oil revenues of Saudi Arabia, Kuwait and the UAE increased from under $2 billion in 1969 to over $48 billion in 1978 – a twenty-five fold increase. It set in motion a process whereby the Gulf region, thanks to its financial wealth, began shifting the balances of power in the Arab world in its favor. As will be seen, this also led to spread of the particular Islamist ideology prevailing in the Gulf at the time.

The Long 1980s and the Rise of Wahhabism

At the heart of Saudi Arabia's emergence as a modern state was the significant tensions between the pragmatic dynasty of al-Saud, and the zealous followers of Saudi Arabia's austere Wahhabi tradition. This tension was on display at multiple times during the consolidation of the Saudi state. The Wahhabi zealots fumed at Ibn Saud's dealing with foreign powers, or even his decision to allow his son to travel abroad. To the Wahhabis, all non-Wahhabis were non-believers, meaning they frequently approached other Muslims with a demand they "accept Islam." This level of extremism was not helpful to the building of the Saudi monarchy, and the tensions between the monarchy and the zealots culminated in the repression of a Wahhabi revolt in 1929. Still, the Saudi monarchy's legitimacy continued to require allegiance to the original 1744 pact between Muhammad ibn Saud and Muhammad ibn Abd al-Wahhab – and thus provided the Wahhabi clergy with a strong position. Until 1979, however, the Saudi rulers had largely managed to confine the influence of the Wahhabi clergy. But the combination of the Iranian revolution and the fallout from the siege of the Grand Mosque pushed Saudi Arabia in an increasingly extremist direction.

More broadly, an Islamist revival had been building in the 1970s. It was a result, in part, of the gradual decline of the appeal of Arab socialist ideology following the Arab armies' defeat in the 1967 war against Israel. In the vacuum that ensued, Islamism gradually emerged as the dominant ideological force. In Saudi Arabia, it took the shape of the *Sahwa* movement, Arabic for awakening, which resulted from the influence of Muslim Brotherhood figures that had migrated to the Kingdom from the 1950s onward from other Arab states where they were repressed. In Saudi Arabia, they became influential in the education system and beyond, and their impact led to a cross-pollination of Saudi Wahhabi ideas with the social and political activism of the Brotherhood. Leading among the ideologists of this movement was Sayid Qutb's brother Muhammad, who spent his life in exile in Saudi Arabia making his late brother's works available to the world while working to reconcile those ideas with the Salafism prevalent in the Kingdom.

Then, in the late 1970s, the Iranian revolution had a massive impact on the broader region, and the radical shift in Iranian policy had a major effect on Saudi Arabia. As fellow monarchs, the Shah and the Sauds had had disagreements on concrete policy issues and a managed rivalry, but were firmly *status quo* powers in the Gulf. This changed with Khomeini, whose notion of an Islamic Republic had appeal far beyond the borders of Iran. The Iranian revolution emboldened the Shi'a minority in Saudi Arabia, leading its members to publicly challenge the prohibitions on Shi'a rituals in the Kingdom in November 1979. This led to rioting that was violently suppressed by the Saudi National Guard.

Iranian rhetoric began to assail the monarchies all over the Arab world and particularly the Saudis as un-Islamic and corrupt. This, in turn, led the Saudis and other Gulf Kingdoms to respond by depicting the Iranian revolution as a purely Shi'a phenomenon, and to that, a *Persian* Shi'a phenomenon. The Saudis also raised their commitment to their own religious doctrine – the vehemently anti-Shia doctrine of the Wahhabis. As Dilip Hiro puts it in his book *Cold War in the Islamic World*, "the Saudi Kingdom entered into a race with the Islamic Republic of Iran as to who was more Islamic than the other."[19]

Almost simultaneously with the Shi'a uprising in the Eastern province, the Saudi Kingdom faced an even greater challenge to its legitimacy. A group of Wahhabi extremists laid siege to the Grand Mosque in Mecca and demanded the Saudi leaders implement the purist Wahhabi doctrine in full. To make matters worse, the official Wahhabi clergy was highly ambivalent to the siege. Leading clerics seemed to think that the militants' might have applied the wrong methods, but that their demands were in fact quite reasonable. Only after obtaining far-reaching pledges to follow Wahhabi doctrine more closely did the clergy give the government religious approval to break the siege by force of arms.

In the years that followed, the Kingdom officially embraced ever more Wahhabi tenets. This included banning pictures of women from newspapers and television, shutting down cinemas, enforcing the segregation of the sexes, and doubling down on the amount of religious indoctrination in schools. Furthermore, the Saudis sought increasingly to export religious extremism by bankrolling Salafi projects around the world. Some of these were

---

19   Dilip Hiro, *Cold War in the Islamic World: Saudi Arabia, Iran and the Struggle for Supremacy*, London: Hurst Publishers, 2018.

supported directly by the Saudi state, while the more controversial and jihadi causes were supported largely by private foundations and individuals within the extensive royal family, which had grown to number into the thousands.

The surge in support for Salafi groups was not limited to Saudi Arabia. It was happening in other Gulf Emirates as well, Kuwait prominent among them. Here, in addition to the factors at work in Saudi Arabia, the rulers were motivated also by the growth of the Muslim Brotherhood as a political force in the country. Unlike the revolutionary Brotherhood supporters, Salafi groups tended to be loyal to the rulers, and this led the ruling family to support Salafis in order to divide adherents of Islamism and thus weaken the potential opposition from the Brotherhood.

The wider Gulf region also faced the challenge of dealing with Iraq, a home to ancient civilizations but also at the time the most powerful revolutionary regime in the Arab world. Ruled by the brutal and mercurial Saddam Hussein, Baghdad saw the Islamic revolution in Iran as an even bigger threat than the Gulf monarchies did. For Iraq, the main problem was not the anti-monarchic character of the new Iranian regime but its virulent Shi'a Islamism. Shi'as formed a majority in Iraq, but the country's rulers had traditionally been drawn from among the region's Sunni Arabs, who represented less than a quarter of the population. Seeing the potential appeal of the Iranian Ayatollahs to Iraq's Shi'as, Saddam Hussein launched an invasion of Iran in September 1980. Instead of a short war that would lead Khomeini's regime to crumble, the invasion allowed Khomeini to rally the nation around him, strengthened his position in Iran, and the war lasted for eight years. Saudi Arabia and the Gulf monarchies bankrolled Iraq's war, in the hope of rolling back Iranian ambitions in the Gulf. Tables would turn very soon after, however, when Iraq sought to annex Kuwait in August 1990. Gulf monarchies now came to the assistance of their fellows in Kuwait, aligning with the United States to force Iraq out of Kuwait.

In sum, the "long 1980s" saw a collapse of the security arrangements in the broader Gulf region. The rise of revolutionary Iran, and of an unpredictable Iraq, followed the departure of the British from the Gulf Emirates. The United States emerged as the new regional hegemon only toward the end of the 1980s, and this role was formalized only with the war over Kuwait in 1990.

The Rise and Fall of Saudi Islamism

In an October 2017 interview with *The Guardian*, Saudi Crown Prince Muhammad bin Salman decried the extremism that had gripped his country for thirty years, and pledged to revert to "a moderate Islam open to the world and all religions." In his analysis, the turn to extremism was "not normal," but a result of the Kingdom's reaction to the Iranian revolution. "We didn't know how to deal with it. And the problem spread all over the world. Now is the time to get rid of it."[20]

This startling admission, coupled with a pledge to rapidly eradicate extremist ideology in the kingdom, was followed by action. Saudi Arabia abolished its religious police, and revoked some of the most regressive legislation, particularly that which governed the segregation of sexes and discrimination against women. The shift in Saudi policy also had international ramifica-

---

20   Martin Chulov, "I Will Return Saudi Arabia to Moderate Islam, Says Crown Prince," *Guardian*, October 24, 2017.

tions: the spigot of Saudi money reaching Islamist causes around the world was summarily turned off. In 2020 Muhammad al-Issa, the new Head of the Muslim World League – a Saudi-led organization that had been a nexus of global Islamism – visited the site of the Auschwitz concentration camp, and stated publicly that the world had to ensure such "horrible crimes never happened again."[21]

The Gulf monarchies' turnaround regarding political Islam did not begin with Muhammad bin Salman – it had been a long time in the making. As mentioned, the Saudi monarchy's approach to religious affairs has on the whole been pragmatic. It had to account for the influence of the Wahhabi clergy in the country, while also working repeatedly to tame the extremism in Wahhabi ranks when those extremists threatened the interests of the monarchy.

During the Cold War, the Saudis saw Arab socialism and world communism as the main threat to the Kingdom's security. And in lockstep with the United States, the Gulf monarchs viewed religion as a key force in resisting the appeal of Arab nationalism and Arab socialism. It is for this reason, more than anything, that the monarchies accommodated thousands of members of the Muslim Brotherhood as they fled from Egypt following Nasser's 1954 crackdown on the movement after a failed assassination attempt on the Egyptian leader. These exiles provided an educated labor force that was direly missing in the Gulf, and Brotherhood figures thus came to occupy influential positions in the education, health and managerial professions across the Gulf states.

The presence of the Brotherhood elites in the Gulf played an

21   Yaakov Schwartz, "This Must Never Happen Again, Says Saudi Cleric as Muslim Group Tours Auschwitz," *Times of Israel*, January 24, 2020.

important role in the rise of modern jihadi ideology. On one hand, the Brotherhood itself had radicalized following Nasser's crackdown, the trajectory of ideologue Sayyid Qutb being a primary example. While in prison, Qutb penned increasingly extremist diatribes that targeted the authoritarian rulers of Muslim states. Among other, he denounced Muslims that opposed the Brotherhood's vision as infidels, thus opening the door for the modern jihadi practice of *takfir*, whereby extremist groups take the liberty of excommunicating other Muslims and thus legitimizing their killing. But beyond that, the Brotherhood was an inherently political movement, consisting of lay people rather than Islamic clerics, organized around the single aim of creating a Caliphate uniting the world's Muslims.

At first, this contrasted starkly with the Wahhabi tradition of the Arabian peninsula. While the Wahhabis were extremely austere in their understanding of religion, they traditionally pledged loyalty to the ruler of a Muslim land. Over time, however, the Wahhabi theology and the Brotherhood political ideology cross-pollinated, leading to the modern jihadi Salafism that has found its expression in Egyptian Islamic Jihad, Al Qaeda, Islamic State, Boko Haram and innumerable offshoot organizations across the world.

Gulf monarchies, beginning with Saudi Arabia, were slow to understand the danger posed by the growth of this ideology. For long, they were content with manipulating and exporting the phenomenon, particularly as this helped them counter the appeal of the Iranian revolution. But already then, the Saudis were dismayed by the Brotherhood's welcoming of the Iranian revolution. This opened a rift between the monarchy and the Brotherhood that would deepen when the Brotherhood endorsed Saddam Hussein's invasion of Kuwait in 1990.

It was in Afghanistan, however, that Saudi leaders weaponized the Islamist ideology against the Soviet Union. Gradually, however, the Saudis – along with their American and Pakistani allies – lost control of the jihadi forces they had helped create. This is, famously, how Al Qaeda emerged. Osama Bin Laden condemned the Kingdom in no uncertain terms. During the 2000s, an understanding began to develop in Saudi leading circles that the support for Islamist extremism around the globe had backfired and now posed a danger to the Kingdom itself. But in the interim, the Wahhabi clergy had consolidated its influence and itself radicalized, thus raising the cost for the Saudi rulers of confronting the extremism it had allowed to get out of control.

Other Gulf states took highly divergent approaches to the problem. In Kuwait, the reigning al-Sabah family allowed parliamentarism to grow, and permitted the Brotherhood's participation in parliamentary politics. It worked to ensure that the Brotherhood stayed loyal to the monarchy, however. Qatar, as will be seen in chapter 9, is the real outlier, aligning fully with the Brotherhood for a combination of pragmatic and ideological reasons. On the other side of the spectrum is the UAE, where Crown Prince Muhammad Bin Zayed early in his life took a distinct dislike to the Brotherhood and its ambitions. Under his leadership, the UAE has taken the lead in countering the spread of the Brotherhood both within the Emirates and regionally, and the Emirati ruler likely had an influence on his Saudi counterparts in this regard as well.

By the time of the Arab upheavals of 2011, the die was cast: the Saudis and Emiratis developed a twin goal in their foreign policy: countering Iranian ambitions while simultaneously ensuring that Sunni Islamists did not come to power in key Arab states. This informed their approach to Syria, where they both endorsed the more secular forces in the opposition, as well as their approach to Egypt, where they worked to remove the Brotherhood from power. And it informed their approach in Libya, where they supported the anti-Islamist forces led by General Khalifa Haftar.

Saudi Arabia's divorce with Islamist ideology has far-reaching implications for the future of the Arab and Muslim world, as it deprives Islamist groupings not only of large subsidies, but of the legitimacy conferred with support from the custodian of the two holy mosques. If this trend continues, and Saudi leaders succeed in launching a modernization program, this could hasten the decline of Islamist ideology globally.

6.
TURKEY'S ENTRY INTO MIDDLE EAST GEOPOLITICS

Turkey's return to an active role in Middle Eastern affairs was perhaps inevitable. Geography, along with religious, cultural and economic linkages dictated that the former imperial power that ruled over much of the region could not turn its back on the Middle East forever. Still, Turkey's active and shifting role in the region has been one of the most important factors in creating the new geopolitics of the Middle East. What this means, however, is not yet clear. Over the past decade, Turkey's relations with Middle Eastern powers has been a roller-coaster, twisting and turning in parallel with Turkey's own domestic political drama. For a time, Turkey pursued a radical and destabilizing agenda; more recently it has tended to side with the Sunni powers against Iran. What is clear is that Turkey's stance will be central to the balance of power in the region for a long time to come.

Cold War Blues

One of Kemalist Turkey's chief objectives was to put distance between Turkey and the Arab Middle East. While Atatürk felt a certain commonality with Pahlavi Iran, the anticlericalism of Kemalist Turkey was considerably more profound than in Iran – as was the country's secularization. The transition to the Latin alphabet and the removal of religious influences on primary education were key facets that led Turkey to mentally step away from the Middle East. As will be seen below, religious conservatives maintained their preference for ties with the Arab world, but the governing elites in Turkey looked almost exclusively to the West. Turkish diplomats, for example, spoke English and French but rarely Arabic or Persian. The Turkish elites viewed the Arab Middle East, in particular, with suspicion, as a region that stabbed the Ottoman Empire in the back when it revolted against Ottoman rule and thus helped to seal the fate of the empire. Ataturk viewed the Arab Middle East as symptomatic of the religious and social backwardness that he wanted Turkey to overcome.

Importantly, this was not a result of an unbridled love for the West. The specter of the Treaty of Sèvres led to a widespread suspicion of Western intentions in Turkey. That Treaty, signed in August 1920, would have ceded large parts of present-day Turkey to Greece, France, and a would-be Armenian state. It would also have put Istanbul and the straits under international control and created British, French and Italian zones of influence over more than half of present-day Turkey. Public reaction to this treaty helped fuel the war of Turkish independence, which brought Atatürk to power. Thus, paradoxically, Turkey's greatest Westernizer came to power as a result of a war against Western powers;

and to this day, a strong suspicion against Western intentions permeates even the most secular portions of Turkish society.

Still, the logic of Atatürk's revolution was fundamentally a Western one. The very embrace of the notion of nationhood, and specifically of a "Turkish" nation instead of an Ottoman monarchy, was a direct product of Western political thought. Similarly, the effort to replace the Sharia with modern, secular law was accomplished through the wholesale importation of entire codes of European law, with minor modifications – the Swiss civil code and the Italian penal code, to be precise. Atatürk himself explained that the West, at the time, represented the "highest level of contemporary civilization." In other words, one could surmise that if the highest level would have been found in China, Turkey would have imported Chinese law instead of European law. This means that Turkey's integration with Europe during the Cold War era was more a pragmatic decision than a deeper identification with European values and norms – an important factor to recall when seeking to understand later changes in Turkey's foreign policy orientation.

The Cold War, which began several years after Atatürk's death in 1938, cemented Turkey's anchoring in Western multilateral institutions. Soviet claims on the Turkish straits, which Stalin voiced at the Yalta and Potsdam conferences in 1945-46, precipitated U.S. security assistance to Turkey and the country's integration into the NATO alliance in 1952. Turkish leaders considered the Soviet threat so serious that they conceded to Western demands for a transition to democratic rule – thus risking their own hold on power. Multi-party democracy was formally introduced in 1946 and the first elections were held in 1950, at which time the conservative opposition led by Adnan Menderes took power. Since then, center-right political forces that were generally pro-Western but more responsive to religious conservatism would dominate Turkish politics. At the time, no one saw any contradiction.

NATO was only one portion of the U.S. effort to contain the Soviet Union. From the early 1950s onward, the U.S. supported the establishment of an alliance seeking to contain the Soviet Union from the south. The Baghdad pact was formally established with members including Turkey, Iraq, Iran, Pakistan and the United Kingdom. The overthrow of the Iraqi monarchy in 1958 led to the withdrawal of Iraq from the alliance, which was renamed the Central Treaty Organization (CENTO) with headquarters moved to Ankara. But CENTO differed from NATO in lacking either an integrated command structure or a clause of mutual defense. While the U.S. was not formally a member of CENTO, the backbone of the pact was the bilateral defense treaties the three member states had with the United States. CENTO survived until the Iranian revolution of 1979, but it failed to prevent a Soviet bid for influence in the Middle East. As seen in previous chapters, while CENTO consisted of non-Arab powers, Moscow established strong relations with Arab countries that embraced a socialist ideology, such as Syria and Egypt.

Turkey kept a measured approach to the many conflicts and controversies in the Middle East. Turkey's priority was to refrain from intervening in Middle Eastern conflicts, and to prevent a scenario where those conflicts came to affect Turkey itself. In other words, Ankara's posture was generally defensive. Thus, Turkey maintained relations with Israel, but simultaneously developed ties with the PLO. It also refrained from taking sides in conflicts between Arab powers, such as those involving Lebanon, Syria, Egypt and Iraq. Turkey's interest in the Middle East also reflected its overall relations with the West. Tensions between Turkey and the West, such as during the 1964 Cyprus crisis or after Turkey's invasion of the island in 1974, led Turkey to look to develop its relationships with Middle Eastern powers, particularly as access to energy resources from the region became more important to Turkey's economy and energy independence.

The relationship with Syria proved particularly significant from a Turkish perspective. Egypt's relations with the Soviet Union collapsed in 1972, leaving Syria as the main Soviet ally in the Middle East. Syria and Turkey had a host of other outstanding issues, including disagreements about sharing the waters of the Euphrates and Tigris rivers, and Turkish allegations of Syrian support for leftist, Armenian and Kurdish exile groups targeting Turkey. Syria, with Soviet approval, provided shelter and support for the Armenian Secret Army for the Liberation of Armenia (ASALA), which conducted over 140 terrorist attacks on Turkish targets in Turkey and abroad from 1973 to 1997. Similarly, Damascus supported the Kurdistan Workers' Party (PKK), headquartered in Lebanon's Bekaa valley and subsequently in Damascus, which emerged in 1978 and began a deadly insurgency against Turkey in 1984. Palestinian groups also coordinated with ASALA. This would become an important factor in bringing about a Turkish-Israeli alignment in the 1990s.

While Turkey had a contentious relationship with Syria, its relationship with Iraq was more ambiguous. As Turkey's trade with the Arab world grew, the main relationships were with oil-producing countries like Saudi Arabia, Libya, and Iraq. The building of a pipeline from Kirkuk in northern Iraq to the Turkish Mediterranean coast cemented the relationship between the two countries; in the 1980s, Turkey and Iraq had a tacit agreement allowing Turkey to pursue Kurdish insurgents several miles into Iraqi territory.

Özal and Reimagining Turkey's Role in the Region

The 1990s would prove a decade of rapid transformation of Turkey's political and economic balance as well as its geopolitical environment. The 1980s had seen the rise of Turgut Özal, a center-right politician with close ties to Turkey's religious conservative circles. Özal rose to power following the end of military rule in 1983, and gained permission from the junta to start a political party that would challenge the bland center-left and center-right parties that the military itself midwifed when it prepared to restore civilian rule.

Voters flocked to Özal's more genuine alternative. In retrospect, Özal was the right man at the right time: of mixed Kurdish and Turkish descent, Özal was respectful of Turkey's secularism while holding the trust of religious circles. A fervent anti-communist, Özal built strong relations with the United States – which at the time endorsed a growing appeal to religion as an antidote to left-wing ideas. Özal also embraced free market thought, and worked to open up Turkey's moribund economy to the world. He proved able to make significant progress in modernizing Turkey's economy. Against this background, Turkey applied for membership in the European Community – the precursor to the European Union – in 1987. Brussels, however, postponed consideration of Turkey's application two years later, citing its lacking political and economic development and poor relations with Greece.

When the Berlin wall fell in 1989, thus, Turkey was in a vulnerable position. Its strategic identity had been clear during the Cold War: aside from Norway, it was the only frontline state that borderied the USSR, providing it with a clear geostrategic role. In the Turkish view, Ankara's contribution to the security of the West should have warranted Western reciprocation by allowing Turkey entry into the economic union being formed in Europe. But the end of the Cold War put an end to hopes of such a *quid pro quo*. And while the collapse of the USSR was in itself a plus, the threat Moscow posed to Turkey had in fact been quite manageable. Turkey's strategic identity was now in flux, and Turkish elites feared that a reduction of the country's importance in Western eyes would doom its bid for full inclusion in the Western community. Worse, Turkey could now be left to its own devices in a region surrounded by troublespots like the Balkans, Caucasus and Middle East.

The first test came with Iraq's annexation of Kuwait in August 1990. Özal jumped on the opportunity to take an important role in the "New World Order" being formed in the aftermath of the Cold War. Moreover, memoirs of high-ranking Turkish officials involved in deliberations at the time confirm that Özal saw an opportunity for Turkey to gain control over territory in northern Iraq. In fact, Atatürk had laid claims to the oil-rich areas around Mosul in northern Iraq, terming them integral parts of the Turkish republic. The British, however, saw Mosul and its oil as necessary for the integrity of Iraq, and the Sunni King Faisal of British-mandate Iraq similarly claimed Mosul, not only for its oil but because its chiefly Sunni Kurdish and Turkic population would reduce the Shi'a dominance of Iraq.

This was the background to Özal's notion that Turkey could benefit from the U.S. war against Iraq to gain control over Mosul, for which Turkey should contribute land forces to the U.S. war effort. But the Turkish General Staff, cautious at heart, was appalled by Özal's adventurism. It followed the Kemalist adage that involvement in Middle Eastern conflicts could only spell trouble for Turkey. In a first, the Chairman of the Turkish General Staff, General Necip Torumtay, resigned (instead of staging a coup, it should be added). A compromise of sorts was reached, whereby Turkey supported the U.S. war on Iraq, provided U.S. use of its airspace and the Incirlik base, but refrained from actively participating in the war.

Özal died of an apparent heart attack in 1993, and after his death Turkey was ruled by unstable coalition governments until Erdogan's AKP came to power in 2002. In the years that followed, the Turkish establishment – including the General Staff – gradually appeared to come around to Özal's way of thinking. The Turkish leadership adapted to a new reality in its neighborhood, with larger elements of uncertainty and a greater need for Turkey to take the initiative. This stemmed in part from the fallout of the Kuwait war: the U.S. did free Kuwait from Iraqi occupation, but refrained from toppling the Iraqi leader, thus leaving Saddam Hussein in power. But the U.S. imposed no-fly-zones over both northern and southern Iraq, which reduced Iraqi sovereignty over the northern areas of the country and created a vacuum where a *de facto* Kurdish state began to emerge.

Meanwhile, Turkey found itself bound by the UN post-war sanctions on Iraq, which led to the closing of the Kirkuk-Ceyhan pipeline for several years. This deprived Turkey of an important source of energy. In addition, Turkey's lucrative trade with Iraq ground to a halt, bringing Turkish losses to an estimated $2 billion per year. More importantly, perhaps, the crippled Iraqi regime was unable to exert authority over the northern areas of the country, and so were the Kurdish self-governing institutions that emerged. Those institutions were not supportive of the PKK, because they consisted mainly of conservative Kurdish forces that abhorred the Marxist-Leninist group. But they were unable to prevent the PKK from establishing bases in northern Iraq from which it launched raids into Turkish territory, thus greatly exacerbating the insurgency's death toll in Turkey.

Turkey responded to this deteriorating security situation in several inter-related ways, which signaled taking a more direct role in Middle Eastern affairs. First, the Gulf War had led Turkey to consider the state of its military and found it was in dire need of modernization to cope with present and future regional challenges. This led to the declaration in 1996 that the Turkish military would spend upwards of $150 billion to modernize its arsenal, a program the fruits of which have begun to be apparent in recent years. Second, Turkey concluded that it could no longer address the PKK insurgency simply through a defensive approach, but needed to shift to a proactive approach that required targeting the sources of PKK support in Syria and Iraq.

During the early 1990s, Turkey retooled its military to fight the PKK in Iraq itself. Starting in 1995, Turkey began launching large-scale ground operations into northern Iraq to take out PKK bases there and displace the actual fighting from Turkish to Iraqi soil. While this gradually helped Ankara get a hold on the situation, it was not a sufficient condition as long as Syria remained a sponsor of the PKK. In this, Turkey and Israel had a strong commonality of interest, which both sides had long been aware of. However, hopes for Arab support on the Cyprus question as well as significant popular support for the Palestinian cause in Turkish public opinion led Turkey to what David Ben-Gurion called a "mistress syndrome," that is to say, an unwillingness to publicize the extent of its relations with Israel.

By the 1990s, Ankara had come to recognize that the Arabs would not come round to support Turkey anyway, and the Oslo peace accords suddenly made it possible to develop ties with Israel without triggering a public opinion backlash. As a result, from 1996 onward Turkey and Israel embarked on a strategic alignment that served several purposes for the Turkish side. First, it provided Turkey with access to Israeli weaponry and intelligence cooperation. Second, it provided Turkey with significant goodwill in the pro-Israeli lobby in the United States, which saw an important strategic interest for both the United States and Israel in the Turkish-Israeli alignment, and led it to come to Turkey's defense and in effect counterbalance the Armenian and Greek lobbies in Congress. Finally, it cornered Syria's Hafiz al Assad, who was left wondering how deep the Turkish-Israeli relationship really was – Turkish General Çevik Bir once compared it to an iceberg, only a fraction of which is visibly above the surface of the water.

As a result, Turkey was able to pressure Syria into submission. After a series of verbal threats in September 1998, Turkey massed troops on the Syrian border and threatened to intervene unless Damascus ceased providing support to the PKK and sanctuary to its leader, Abdullah Öcalan. By mid-October, al-Assad relented, as Syria was unprepared for the prospect of a possible conflict on two fronts with both Turkey and Israel. This led to the Mossad's capture of Öcalan at the Greek Embassy in Nairobi in February 1999 and his handover to Turkish intelligence.

As can be seen, the second half of the 1990 saw a more direct Turkish engagement with Middle Eastern affairs in order to safeguard the country's security and ultimately its territorial integrity. At this time, in spite of Turkish dissatisfaction with U.S. policies in Iraq and Turkish concerns with the emergence of a Kurdish *de facto* state there, successive Turkish governments saw the country's interests as best served by a continuous engagement with the United States and a strategic alignment with Israel. This policy paid immediate dividends, leading Turkey to capture the country's public enemy no. 1, and to bring the PKK insurgency to a temporary halt.

A decade later, however, these advances had been undone, and Turkey had embarked on a very different trajectory. This was in part a response to regional events, but more importantly a result of Turkish domestic shifts. In fact, Turkey's approach to the Middle East – and to world politics more generally – has been directly dependent on the ideological outlook of various Turkish political movements. A quick overview of these differences will help understand the shifts and swerves in Turkish approaches to the region.

Ideology and Politics in Turkey

Samuel P. Huntington famously declared that Turkey was a "Torn Country" – culturally and socially divided between groups in society that agreed on very little in terms of what their country should look like, what threats it faces, where its allegiances lies, and the direction of its foreign policy.

During the Cold War, a left-right dimension dominated Turkish politics. The "left," which remained in a minority position in a generally center-right country, questioned the prevailing capitalist order and was skeptical of relations with the West, while more radical groups supported the Soviet Union. Because the "right" was associated with the dominant Sunni Muslim and ethnically Turkish majority, the left tended to attract members of minority groups disenchanted with the dominant order. This is a reason why the main expression of Kurdish nationalism in Turkey has been virulently left-wing, and why the heterodox Alevis have tended to support the left as well. As for the "right," this large and relatively amorphous group included everything from center-right liberal and democratic forces, to ethnic nationalists and Islamic conservatives. What these forces all had in common was their support for the free market, and their agreement that the Soviet Union and communism were the biggest threats to Turkey. This in turn led them to welcome, indeed promote, the alliance with the United States. While it may seem counterintuitive today that Islamic conservatives would support the United States, this made sense in the Cold War context. It should be recalled that the U.S., during the 1980s, supported the rise of political Islam in Turkey as a counter-force to the Communist threat –while also supporting the Islamist leader Zia ul-Haq in Pakistan and channeling weapons to the mujahideen in Afghanistan.

With the end of the Cold War, the left-right split ceased to dominate Turkish society. Gradually, instead, the chief dividing lines came to be related to identity. Thus, one prominent divide in the country was between the portion of the population that was urban, modern, and European in outlook and lifestyle; and that which was more traditional, conservative, and Islamic. Superimposed on this was the divide between the majority Turks and a large portion of the Kurdish minority which maintained an emphasis on a separate Kurdish identity.

Politically, divergences emerged between centrists, Islamists and nationalists. While all were accommodated in the Democratic Party of the 1950s and 60s, they then gradually split up into rivaling political parties. All found room, to some degree and in competition with each other, in the ruling coalitions led by Turgut Özal in the late 1980s, and then again under Erdogan's leadership in the 2000s.

Up until the 2000s, the dominant force in the Turkish right was the centrist view, personified by the likes of Turgut Özal and Süleyman Demirel. Centrists emphasized the importance of Turkey's ties to the West, the primacy of NATO, and the objective of integration with the European Union. They came increasingly to approve of Turkish involvement in the Middle East, but did so either because of national security concerns, involving primarily threats emerging from Syria, Iraq and Iran; or to support Turkish business ties with markets in the Middle East. There was no romanticism about the Middle East among Turkish centrists, who generally tended to have unfavorable views of Arabs.

Turkey's nationalists have historically been more averse to integration with the West than the centrists, but their virulent anti-Communism led them to support Turkey's alliance with the United States. Nationalists stand out by their emphasis on ties with the Turkic states of Central Asia and Azerbaijan, a heavy antipathy toward Iran, and an aversion for the Arab Middle East. They have also been driven to a considerable degree by animosity toward traditional Turkish foes like Russia and Greece. Over time, however, a division has taken place among nationalists: a minority view known as the *ulusalcı* or neo-nationalists, hold that the U.S. is the biggest threat to Turkey, and that Turkey should therefore join forces with an anti-western coalition led by Russia and China against the West.

The *ulusalcı* view of the world has gained popularity as a result of America's support for Kurdish groups in Iraq and Syria, and its hosting of exiled preacher Fethullah Gülen, who is held responsible for the 2016 coup attempt. Even though the core *ulusalcı* grouping has remained limited in influence, the under-standing of the United States as a threat to Turkey rather than an ally has spread across the political spectrum. There are two main reasons for this: first, the widely held (but never substantiated) belief that the United States masterminded, or at best was aware of the 2016 coup; and second, the fact that the U.S. has supported Kurdish Syrian guerrillas aligned with the PKK, an organization the U.S. *itself* considers terrorist.

The Islamist and Islamic conservatives, which were the driving force in organizing the AKP, had been at the forefront of anti-Communism during the Cold War, often in alliance with nationalists. But they became increasingly anti-Western as the relationship between the West and the Muslim world soured from the 1990s onward. Islamists urged Turkey to drop its ties with the West and seek, instead, to (once again) be the leader of the Muslim world. Islamists and Islamic conservatives promote an orientation toward the core Arab Middle East, which is the center of Islamic civilization. They are, in other words, the most dedicated supporters of a foreign policy that focuses on the Middle East. But this does not mean there is a consensus on how this would happen in practice: some elements are more sectarian in nature, and oppose Shi'a Iran; while others could be considered more pan-Islamic, emphasizing solidarity across sectarian lines for Muslims to cooperate against the West. In practice, Islamist ideology is connected with support for political Islamic forces across the Middle East, something that has led to a reaction by Arab regimes that see political Islam as a threat.

Thus, Turkey's approach to the Middle East, and its foreign policy in general, has differed greatly depending on the contours of the ruling coalition at the helm of the Turkish state. Importantly, that includes a balance between the elected political power and the unelected guardians of the military and intelligence services of the country.

Political Islam's Moment

Turkey's return to Middle East politics following the end of the Cold War was in many ways a function of the country's security situation and the perception of threats coming from the Middle East. Erdogan's AKP government, by contrast, sought to shift the rationale for this from a negative to a positive one – toning down the threats coming from the region, and instead emphasizing the opportunities. While initially formulated in neutral language, the ideological underpinnings of this initiative soon became clear – as Turkey's support for political Islam increasingly went in lockstep with its attempt to exert influence across the region.

The first years of Erdogan's tenure were focused greatly on Ankara's efforts to start accession talks with the European Union. This effort in itself for a long time masked the AKP government's Islamist origins. After all, if they were Islamists, why would they seek membership in the EU? But in reality, Erdogan's effort to negotiate with the EU was a result of two key rationales: first, to attract Western investors to Turkey's economy; and second and more importantly, to gain leverage from the West to consolidate power, and displace a Kemalist establishment in the military and bureaucracy that was extremely skeptical of Erdogan's Islamist background. In this, Erdogan successfully used the EU as a cudgel to assert civilian control over the military.

But even early on, the signs were there for those looking for them. After Hamas came to power in Gaza in 2006, Turkey wholeheartedly embraced this terrorist organization as legitimate freedom fighters, while Erdogan repeatedly ignored international concern over his closeness to Sudanese ruler Omar al-Bashir, a Brotherhood-connected figure in his own right. Erdogan also promoted Islamist ideologue Ahmet Davutoglu to his main foreign policy advisor. As would become clear after the 2011 Arab upheavals, Erdogan and Davutoglu had marinated in Islamist thinking since their formative years, and perceived the events as meaning the collapse of the Western-led order imposed on the Middle East following the collapse of the Ottoman Empire.

Turkey would emerge as a strong backer of the forces motivated by political Islam that challenged the *status quo* across the Middle East and North Africa.

As will be seen in later chapters in this book, this led to Turkey emerging as a leading backer of the Muslim Brotherhood government in Egypt, as an early supporter of regime change in Syria, and as a direct participant in the conflict over government in Libya. It also put Turkey on collision course with both the Arab monarchies and Israel, who all supported the reigning *status quo* and strongly opposed the rise to prominence of Sunni political Islam across the region. Indeed, Turkey's growing involvement in the region, and its alignment with Qatar, created a new force in Middle Eastern geopolitics that was inherently radical, challenged the *status quo* in ways that helped generate a deep split within the Sunni Muslim world.

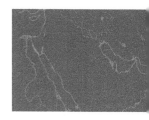

7.
IRAN'S ARC OF DOMINATION

Over the past four decades, the Iranian regime has actively sought to build its influence across the Middle East and beyond through a variety of means. Some of those means are conventional and part of normal international relations, like diplomatic engagement across the region and alignment with other regional powers, such as Russia. But the bulk of Iran's effort has been decidedly unconventional. In fact, Iran has sought to build regional dominance by supporting political and militant groups across the region, including sponsoring outright terrorist groups that have served Iranian purposes. What Iran has sought to build has been called many names: an "axis of resistance" by the Iranians and their allies; a "Shi'a Crescent" according to some. In reality, it is a network of Iranian domination of the region.

This arc reaches from Lebanon in the west across Syria and Iraq all the way to Yemen. As will be seen, efforts to build this network started long ago in Lebanon, but accelerated rapidly after the 2003 U.S. invasion of Iraq and the 2011 Arab Spring, which Iran capitalized upon to extend and solidify its influence. Coupled with the regime's radical ideological agenda, this has been the most dramatic driver of change in the region in the past decade.

Lebanon and Hezbollah

The first theater where revolutionary Iran managed to get a foothold was relatively far-flung, namely in Lebanon. There were several reasons why this tiny country of three million (in the early 1980s) became a priority for Iran. Lebanon is home to a large Shi'a Arab population, which has been the fastest growing religious community in this fragmented country. Whereas Shi'a were estimated at 17 percent in 1921, they rose to over 30 percent of the population by the late 1980s. Because positions of power were divided between the major communities in the Lebanese political system, the country lacked a strong central government. As civil unrest grew in the mid-1970s, revolutionary Iran saw an opportunity to establish a foothold in the Levant, on Israel's doorstep, by becoming the benefactor of the Shi'a community.

Tehran had to contend with the existence of a political movement among the Shi'a in Lebanon called Amal, which was under strong Syrian influence. Yet Amal's religious leaders rejected Khomeini's novel doctrine of Vilayat-e-Faqih, and the movement's more secular character was also anathema to Khomeini. As a result, Iran helped create the Lebanese Hezbollah movement, which was not only loyal to Tehran but recognized Khomeini's religious and temporal authority. Hezbollah grew in stature and power very much as a result of significant Iranian support. Iran has bankrolled the movement with a yearly support estimated to be, on average, in the range of $100 million to $200 million. It has also trained thousands of Hezbollah fighters, and provided large amounts of weaponry to Hezbollah. Iran also helps fund the Al Manar TV station, a major tool for Hezbollah propaganda.

Hezbollah has, however, diversified its sources of funding and is not solely reliant on Iranian support. It has established a sophisticated, global network of organized criminal activities, in particular involving itself in the trafficking of narcotics and weapons as well as money laundering. Through the Lebanese diaspora in Latin America and West Africa, Hezbollah developed close ties with drug trafficking cartels in Colombia and Mexico, and has played an important role in helping transport drug shipments to Europe through West Africa, protecting the shipments, and laundering the proceeds back to the Latin American cartels. Aside from such large-scale trafficking, Hezbollah has been involved in all kinds of smaller criminal operations, such as credit card fraud in the United States and smuggling cigarettes into Canada.

Experts estimate that Hezbollah derives up to 30 percent of its budget from criminal activities, meaning the lion share still comes from Iran. This separate source of income helps Hezbollah derive some level of autonomy from Tehran, though the tie between them is deep and strategic – and definitely goes both ways. Hezbollah leader Hassan Nasrallah's connection in Tehran was directly to Supreme Leader Ali Khamenei, and the two went way back: in 2019, Nasrallah reminisced on Khamenei's direct personal involvement in the creation of Hezbollah in the 1980s.[22] Iran's influence is institutionalized through the presence of two Iranian representatives out of nine members in Hezbollah's highest decision-making council.[23]

Hezbollah's evolution has tracked in parallel with changes in Iran's approach. Tehran at first urged Hezbollah to stay out of Lebanon's sectarian politics, but following the 1989 reconciliation accords, Tehran approved of Hezbollah's intention to take an active part in politics. The accord was, in theory, supposed to dismantle all militia groups in the country in order to restore the state's monopoly over the use of force. However, under the guise of being a "resistance movement" to Israel rather than a militia, Hezbollah was allowed to retain its armed forces.

Over the decades that followed, Hezbollah developed into a state within a state in Lebanon. Iranian support enabled it to strengthen its military force so that it in many ways rivaled Lebanon's official armed forces. And though its representation in parliament was always modest – in recent years it has had about a tenth of the seats – its superior organization and muscle has allowed it to have an outsize influence on Lebanese politics. This influence has also helped alter, somewhat, the relationship between Iran and Hezbollah, as observers now see Tehran deferring to Nasrallah on matters relating to Lebanese domestic politics, rather than trying to impose its own views.[24] There should be

22   "Nasrallah says Khamenei heavily involved in establishment of Lebanon's Hezbollah,"
       Al-Arabiya, October 1, 2019. https://english.alarabiya.net/News/middle-east/2019/10/01/
       Nasrallah-says-Khamenei-heavily-involved-in-establishment-of-Lebanon-s-Hezbollah

23   Eitan Azani, "Hezbollah, a Global Terrorist Organization," Hearing of the House Committee
       on International Relations, Subcommittee on International Terrorism and Nonproliferation,
       September 2006. (https://ict.org.il/hezbollah-a-global-terrorist-organization/)

24   "Becoming Hezbollah: The Party's Evolution and Changing Roles," Brandeis University
       Crown Center, January 27, 2023. https://www.brandeis.edu/crown/publications/crown-
       conversations/cc-16.html

no doubt about the closeness of the relationship, however. Iran's former Ambassador to Lebanon, Ali Akbar Mohtashemi, who helped create Hezbollah, once stated that Hezbollah is "part of the Iranian rulership; a central component of the Iranian military and security establishment."[25]

As will be discussed in detail in subsequent chapters, the Syrian civil war changed matters dramatically for Hezbollah, as the organization was forced to make a rather unpopular choice. It threw its weight behind Bashar al-Assad's regime, and even deployed troops into the Syrian civil war to defend Assad and thus its own lifeline to Iran. While this damaged Hezbollah's reputation and standing in the Arab world, it underscored the centrality of its link to Tehran, which similarly saw the impending demise of Assad as a potentially catastrophic blow to Iranian interests, and specifically to the building of its arc of domination across the region. Along with Iran's own Quds force, Russian support, and a multitude of Iraqi Shi'a militias, Hezbollah played a key role in averting the collapse of Assad's regime, thus handing Iran a major victory in the geopolitical struggles of the past decade.

The Syrian Lynchpin

The Syrian and Iranian regimes may at first sight appear unlikely bedfellows. Syria's Assad regime has its ideological roots in Arab socialism, and its leadership is decidedly secular. The Alawi (also known as Nusayri) sect to which Assad belongs, and which has an outsize influence over the regime, belongs to Shi'a Islam only technically, since they consider Imam Ali an incarnation of God.

---

25   Azani, "Hezbollah's Global Reach."

In practice, Alawism is a syncretistic and mystical belief that has little in common with Iran's Twelver Shi'a Islam. Being non-Sunni, however, they have a common hostility toward extremist Sunni and Salafi versions of Islam.

While this has brought Damascus and Tehran closer in recent years, it was not much of an issue when the relationship between the two began to develop in the 1980s. Instead, the relationship was built on common threat perceptions and common enemies. These common enemies were Iraq, Israel and the United States. Iran's opposition to Iraq is self-explanatory given Saddam Hussein's invasion of Iran in September 1980. Syria and Iraq were both ruled by different wings of the same but notoriously fractious Baath Party, and the enmity between these wings explains the growing rift between Damascus and Baghdad that coincided with the war between Iran and Iraq. Indeed, in July 1979, Saddam Hussein had conducted a massive purge of his ruling Baath Party, blaming the Syrian Baath Party of orchestrating a coup against him. To all appearances, this was a way to remove his detractors within the Iraqi elite and assert power. This led Syria, as virtually the only Arab state, to support Iran during the Iran-Iraq war.

As for Israel, Syria had always been a leading force in the anti-Israel Arab coalition, and the Iranian revolutionaries' enmity to Israel brought the two further together. As a Soviet-supported regime, Assad stood in opposition to the United States, which was Israel's main supporter – but his opposition to the U.S. was by no means as deeply ideologically rooted as it was in Iran. Still, these common perspectives on regional matters brought Damascus and Iran together, at first as a relationship of near-equals, in spite of Iran's much larger size. During the 1980s, Damascus and

Tehran cooperated on regional issues but did not see eye to eye on everything. In Lebanon, they at first supported different protégés among Lebanon's Shi'a, but following the 1989 accords, Syria and Iran managed to join forces, and solidify the cooperation between the Hezbollah and Amal factions.

The relationship gained further ground in the mid-2000s, following the U.S. invasion of Iraq. While that did away with Saddam Hussein, it led both Assad and Khamenei to fear American designs on them, and soon after Syria was forced to withdraw its forces from Lebanon after a popular revolt there dubbed the "Cedar Revolution." Israel's war with Hezbollah in 2006 further brought Tehran and Damascus together, with the balance between them shifting in Iran's favor. This tilt grew even stronger after the Arab Spring revolts of 2011, with the ascendancy of Sunni extremism and ISIS across the region. Iran bet the farm on saving the Assad regime from collapsing. At a time when most in the Sunni Arab world, Turkey and the West anticipated a rapid collapse of the regime, Iran pulled out all stops to invest heavily in maintaining Assad in power. Not staying at that, it was reportedly IRGC Quds Forces commander Qassem Soleimani who, in July 2015, convinced Russia that Assad would fall unless Moscow stepped in to back up the Iranian effort to bolster the regime.[26]

In recent years, Tehran had capitalized on the U.S. debacle in Iraq to build friendly forces in Iraqi government and politics, and succeeded in building a logistical link linking Iran to Syria and Lebanon across Iraq. Losing Syria would have obliterated

---

26   Laila Bassam and Tom Perry, "How Iranian general plotted out Syrian assault in Moscow," Reuters, October 6, 2015. (https://www.reuters.com/article/us-mideast-crisis-syria-soleimani-insigh-idUSKCN0S02BV20151006)

this strategic accomplishment in Iran's efforts to establish its regional domination.

Instead, Iran doubled down and achieved a major victory. Not only did it sustain Assad in power, but it gained enormous influence inside Syria. This influence is first and foremost military, as Iran deployed Shi'a militias, Hezbollah, the Quds force, and regular IRGC forces into the Syrian civil war. According to one estimate, Iran has over 130 military sites in Syria that it controls directly or indirectly, with over 100,000 forces belonging to more than seventy different militia groups.[27] To this should be added Iran's growing influence over Syria's regular army, particularly the fourth division commanded by Maher al-Assad, the President's brother, as well as Syrian intelligence.

Iran's influence does not end with military and security affairs, but extends to an attempt to fundamentally remake the demographic structure of Syria. As is well-known, the civil war resulted in a massive outflow of primarily Sunni Syrians. This is no coincidence, as it was the Sunnis that coalesced into the bulk of the opposition to the Assad regime. Jointly, the Syrian and Iranian regimes have embarked on an effort to shift Syria's demography through suppressing Sunni identity and bolstering the Shi'a, through a variety of means that, in the long term, will make Syria a very different country than it was before 2011. To begin with, Iran has encouraged Shi'a militiamen from other countries – Iraq, Afghanistan or Pakistan – who fought in Syria to bring their families, settling in homes formerly belonging to

---

27   Ido Yahel, "Iran in Syria: From Expansion to Entrenchment," Moshe Dayan Center, Tel Aviv Notes, June 17, 2021. (https://dayan.org/content/iran-syria-expansion-entrenchment); Middle East Media Monitoring Institute, "Report By London-Based Saudi Magazine Details Names, Numbers, Locations Of Iran-Backed Militias In Syria, Particularly Near Israeli Border," November 9, 2023. (https://www.memri.org/jttm/report-london-based-saudi-magazine-details-names-numbers-locations-iran-backed-militias-syria)

Sunni Syrians. In addition, Iran has launched a major campaign to convert Sunnis in Syria to the Shi'a sect, through a mixture of missionary activity, humanitarian assistance, and outright intimidation. The extent of the success of this venture remains to be determined, but the scope of the effort is monumental.

While the secular Assad regime has little interest in Tehran's theology, Iran saved the regime, and as long as its own lifestyle is not in danger, the regime appears to care little whether the price of staying in power is a "Shi'ification" of Syria. Iran may have invested up to $100 billion in Syria since the beginning of the civil war, and appears, for now, to have successfully turned Syria into a vassal state.[28]

Making Iraq Subservient

Forming the two largest countries with Shi'a Muslim majorities, Iran and Iraq have been closely interlinked for centuries. The Iranian city of Qom and the Iraqi city of Najaf are the two central sites of Shi'a learning, and pilgrims from Iran have plowed the roads leading to the main Shi'a holy sites which are in Iraq. More recently, of course, the two countries' modern history has been plagued by the nearly decade-long Iran-Iraq war, which was truly a formative experience for the Iranian regime.

Under the Shah, relations had been complicated but manageable. This changed with Saddam Hussein's onslaught and the eight years of vicious warfare that ensued. Iraq continued to be a major focus for the leaders of the Iranian regime long after

---

28   Rauf Baker, "Tehran's Shiification of Syria; Iran's Hegemonic Drive," *Middle East Quarterly*, Winter 2023. (https://www.meforum.org/middle-east-quarterly/pdfs/63851.pdf); Amatzia Baram, "Iran's stakes in Syria," GIS Reports, October 28, 2021 (https://www.gisreportsonline.com/r/iran-syria/).

the war, as they continued to see Iraq as a most direct threat against Iran. The U.S. invasion of Iraq in 2003 at first generated enormous fears in Iran, coming so soon after the U.S. defeated the Taliban in Afghanistan and established a military presence in that country. This "sandwiching" between U.S. forces – who now practically encircled Iran – led Tehran to fear that it could be attacked next. This prospect was not entirely unrealistic, given the presence of influential forces in the Bush Administration that wanted to do just that. But the U.S. Iraq war did not go according to plan, and the missteps of the U.S. opened an opportunity for Iran to step in and work not only to counter the U.S. presence in Iraq, but to assert its own influence in the vacuum created by the United States.

In this regard, the U.S. decision to dismantle the Iraqi military under the guise of "de-Baathification" in one stroke gutted the key state institutions of the country, leaving a giant vacuum that the U.S. itself was unable to fill. While the decision was justifiable on ethical grounds given the past brutality of the Baathist regime, it instantly created several hundred thousand adversaries for the United States, and kickstarted the process of building a Sunni resistance to the U.S. occupation.

The U.S. leadership also made a serious miscalculation regarding the Iraqi Shi'a. Seeing Sunni extremism personified by Al Qaeda as the most direct threat to America, and viewing Saudi Arabia increasingly as a liability because of its sponsorship of Salafi groups worldwide, thinkers in the Bush Administration conceived of the oppressed Shi'a majority in Iraq as the centerpiece of a new American strategy for the Middle East. The Iraqi Shi'a were expected to be agents of democratization not only in

Iraq itself but across the region, and thus a pro-American Iraq run by its Shi'a majority would be the new lynchpin of America's presence in the region.

This theory ignored that Iran would have much greater leverage on Iraq and particularly the Iraqi Shi'a following the demise of the Baath party. Most Iraqi Shi'a leaders had been in exile in Iran (perhaps 200,000 had sought refuge there) and though there were differences in outlook between many Iraqi groups and Tehran, Iran was incomparably better networked and had a staying power and understanding of Iraqi realities that America simply could not compete with. It put America in the strange situation that the community, and leaders, that the U.S. sought to make the vehicle for its influence in the region were the same that its main regional adversary, Iran, had close affinities with and, in some cases, had sponsored for years. Thus, Iran developed a network of politicians it supported, providing Iran with an influence on the Iraqi parliament and in turn, influence over the formation of governments.

While Iran, as in Syria, has sought to breed support across sectarian lines by cultural and humanitarian efforts, at the end of the day the core of Iran's policy – just like it does at home – rests on violence and suppression. From the outset, Iran has trained, funded and organized a variety of primarily Shi'a Arab militias in Iraq, which played a direct role in violence against American forces in Iraq. Iranian arms factories produced roadside bombs known as Explosively Formed Penetrators (EFP) that were delivered by the thousands to insurgents led and trained by the IRGC Quds force and Lebanese Hezbollah. Iran also provided a host of other weapons, including armor-penetrating sniper rifles purchased from Austria, to Iraqi insurgents. All in all, British and American officials estimate that Iran was responsible for over 1,000 American deaths in Iraq and a much larger number of wounded. Similarly in Afghanistan, Iran and the Taliban temporarily overcame their sectarian differences against their common enemy, allowing the IRGC Quds Force to train Taliban fighters, and even to pay them a prize for every American soldier they killed.[29]

These Iranian-supported militias in Iraq also form a significant part of the so-called Popular Mobilization Forces, created in 2014 as an attempt to coordinate the militias fighting against the Islamic State. Some of these militias are loyal to Iran's rivals such as Ayatollah Al-Sistani and Moqtada al-Sadr, and all are nominally loyal to the government of Iraq. In reality, however, these militias operate autonomously and those under Iran's influence follow the instructions of the IRGC rather than the Iraqi government.

Iraqi society, including Iraqi Shi'ites, are by no means uniformly pro-Iranian. In fact, Iraqi views on Iran have fluctuated considerably in the past two decades – being at the highest when Iran stepped in to confront the Islamic State, and at its lowest when Iran has appeared to intervene with a heavy hand in Iraqi politics. One survey has favorable views of Iran fluctuating from 26 to 86 percent over this period.[30] While common Shi'a identity and opposition to Sunni extremism bind Iran and Iraq together, the presence, and rise, of Iraqi nationalism is an important factor undermining Iranian influence. Still, there is a consensus that no

---

29 Richard Kemp and Chris Driver-Williams, "Killing Americans and their Allies: Iran's Continuing War against the United States and the West," Jerusalem Center for Public Affairs, 2015. (https://jcpa.org/pdf/Kemp.pdf)

30 Jessica Watkins, "Iran in Iraq," LSE Middle East Center, Papers Series no. 27, 2020, p. 12. (https://eprints.lse.ac.uk/105768/4/Iran_in_Iraq.pdf)

Iraqi leader can come to power without the tacit acceptance of Tehran. Iraq has on several occasions seen protest movements directed in part against Iran, opposing Iranian influence on the country's government. This happened in 2011, for example, but much larger demonstrations that were often explicitly anti-Iranian took place in late 2019. Responding to these demonstrations that threatened the pro-Iranian government in the country, the Iran-aligned militias stepped in (allegedly with little coordination with the Iraqi government) and repressed the demonstrations with force, including killing scores of protestors. These militias also used the general chaos to attack the American embassy in Baghdad, prompting the U.S. to retaliate by killing the legendary Quds Force commander Qassem Soleimani, who allegedly orchestrated the attack on the Embassy, near Baghdad airport in January 2020.

Killing this charismatic and legendary commander of Iran's regional power projects was a strong blow to Iran, but did not change the fact that Iran remains firmly entrenched in Iraq, and has proven willing to engage in significant repression of anti-Iranian forces in Iraq to maintain this influence.

Yemen: Iran's Underestimated Role

The latest addition to the Iranian axis of domination is Yemen, where the Iranian regime has thrown its weight behind the Ansar Allah group, more widely known as the Houthi movement. The impact of this relationship was frontline news in early 2024, when Houthi forces targeted civilian shipping that it deemed associated with Israel in the Red Sea, leading the U.S. and UK to respond with airstrikes.

The Houthis draw support from among the Zaidi community, who account for around a third to two fifths of Yemen's population. The Zaidis are nominally an offshoot of Shi'ism, although
they are a separate branch from the Twelver Shi'a of Iran. In this
sense, Iran's approach to them is similar to its relationship with
the Alawis in Syria. Being nominally Shi'a and opposed to Sunni
powers like Saudi Arabia is enough for Iran to embrace the movement in its quest for regional domination.

Surprisingly, the U.S. government and major analytical organizations like the Rand Corporation long took a rather cautious,
if not skeptical approach, to the Iranian influence over the Houthi
movement. Iranian support has been seen as opportunistic and
rather recent.[31] However, considerable evidence suggests the Iranian link to the Houthis is in fact organic and deep-seated.[32]

The Houthi movement originates with Badraddin al-
Houthi, a preacher from the Sa'ada province of northern Yemen.
The Houthi family belongs to a branch of the Zaidi Shi'a known
as the Jarudi, which agree with the twelver Shi'a that only Ali's
lineage had the right to succeed the prophet. In other words,
like the twelver Shi'a, Jarudi Zaidis consider the first successor
Caliphs to be illegitimate. This, at the outset, created a theological
alignment with Iranian Shi'a. Badruddin al-Houthi and his sons
were immediate cheerleaders for the Iranian revolution, not least
because it showed a level of political activism that they viewed as
more common among the Zaidis than among the twelver Shi'a.

---

31   Barak Salmoni, Bryce Loidolt, and Madeleine Wells, *Regime and Periphery in Northern
     Yemen: The Huthi Phenomenon*, Santa Monica: RAND, 2010. Also State Department reports
     published wikileaks.

32   See Oved Lobel, *Becoming Ansar Allah: How the Islamic Revolution Conquered Yemen*, European
     Eye on Radicalization, Report no. 20, March 2021. (https://kyleorton1991.files.wordpress.
     com/2024/01/ansar-allah-iran-report-oved-lobel.pdf)

One Houthi leader explained to a researcher that there may be minor theological differences between the (Jarudis) Zaidis and the twelvers, but that "politically we are identical."[33]

Badruddin and his son Huseyn spent time in Iran in the early 1980s and subsequently traveled frequently there, as well as to Lebanon, where they built relations with Lebanese Hezbollah. They helped create a youth organization called "Believing Youth" in the early 1990s, and thousands of young Yemenis went through the group's summer camps. In addition, the Houthis sent forty students a year to Iranian seminaries in Qom from 1994 to 2014.[34] Houthi literature disseminated at camps featured Hezbollah luminaries such as Hassan Nasrallah, and this slide in the direction of Iranian-promoted theology and political ideology led to criticism from traditional Zaidi authorities that the Houthis had become surrogates for Iranian twelver Shi'a beliefs.

Thus, from the 1980s onward, there is clear evidence that Iran was copying the Hezbollah model in Yemen, gradually building a pro-Iranian constituency in this strategic country on the approaches to the Suez Canal, and flanking its rival Saudi Arabia from the south.

This movement, building during the 1990s, was then activated in the early 2000s following the 9/11 attacks and America's greater engagement with the broader region. Yemen's president Ali Abdullah Saleh sided firmly with the United States. After Huseyn al-Houthi, son of Badruddin, returned in the late 1990s

---

33   Mahdi Khalaji, "Yemen's Zaidis: A Window for Iranian Influence," Washington Institute for Near East Policy, Policy Watch 2364, February 2, 2015. (https://www.washingtoninstitute.org/policy-analysis/yemens-zaidis-window-iranian-influence)

34   Michael Knights, Adnan al-Garbani, and Casey Coombs, "The Houthi Jihad Council: Command and Control in 'the Other Hezbollah," CTC Sentinel, October 2022. (https://www.washingtoninstitute.org/media/5910)

from exile in Iran and Sudan (which at the time was a center of IRGC operations)[35] a schism within the movement occurred. Al-Houthi created a militant faction that utilized the motto used by the Houthi movement today: "God is Great! Death to America! Death to Israel! A Curse on the Jews! Victory to Islam!" As is clear from this slogan, al-Houthi's political movement focuses a lot on the broader pan-Islamist agenda promoted by the Iranian regime, rather than local concerns. In particular, the obsession with the Jews and Israel, visible then as it is now, has little connection to Yemeni realities. Even the timing of the war between the Houthis and Yemen, beginning in 2004, connects to the U.S. invasion of Iraq and Iran's efforts to counter American presence in the region.

The Houthis and the Yemeni government would fight intermittently from 2004 to 2011. Following the Arab Upheavals of 2011, however, Yemen's situation deteriorated and from 2014 transitioned into a protracted and bloody civil war that has dragged in neighboring powers. Iran rapidly expanded its support for the Houthis, and after the Houthis began making incursions into Saudi territory, Saudi and Emirati forces stepped in to decimate the Houthis and strengthen the official government of Yemen. The intervention nevertheless failed, not least because Iran continuously raised the stakes. Once the Houthis captured the capital Sana'a, and not least the main port infrastructure on Yemen's west coast, Iran was able to greatly expand its delivery of weapons to the Houthis, enabling them to consolidate control over the rump Yemeni state. In other words, Iran engineered a scenario very similar to the one in Lebanon.

35   Amira Mohammad Abdulhalim, "Iranian Revolutionary Guard Corps' Influence in Africa Intensive Interventions and Challenges," *Journal of Iranian Studies*, vol. 2 no. 6, 2018.

Conclusions

The Iranian arc of domination has developed immensely in the past two decades. The 2003 Iraq war enabled Iran to assert influence over that country, whereas the Arab Upheavals of 2011 paved the way for Iranian control over Syria and the Houthi government in Yemen. This put all Middle East powers on notice, and all are reacting to this bid for hegemony on behalf of the most populous power in the region, to that one that is developing nuclear weapons. Others therefore have vacillated between confronting and appeasing Iran. During the Trump administration in particular, there was a sense that America had the backs of countries seeking to block Iran's expansionist agenda. With the Biden Administration and the return of officials that had advocated for the Iran nuclear deal, several Gulf states instead moved toward seeking some form of reduction of tensions with Iran. But the basic outlines of the key geopolitical confrontation in the region remains: Iran is the driving force, and others are reacting to it.

8.
TURKEY, QATAR, AND THE BROTHERHOOD AXIS

In the 2010s, a second attempt to unseat the status quo across the Middle East emerged alongside Iran's long-standing efforts to establish an arc of domination. This time, it came from the Sunni world. Following the Arab upheavals of 2011, Turkey and Qatar embarked on an effort to support the spread of governments built on the ideology of the Muslim Brotherhood. This effort drove a deep wedge through the Sunni Arab world, and had wide-ranging geopolitical implications. This strange alliance between a non-Arab power, an ambitious Arab micro-state and a transnational network perplexed many, including Western policymakers. Was this a democratic force seeking to unseat authoritarian rulers, or a dangerous Islamist group bent on its own form of hegemony? Many were led to believe the former answer to be true, but developments would suggest otherwise.

When the Arab social and political upheavals hit in 2011, a sort of euphoria spread across Western officialdom and newsrooms. Democracy was finally coming to the Middle East. However, it soon became clear that the main beneficiary across the region would be Islamist groups, most of which formed part of the Muslim Brotherhood's network. This was obviously the case in Egypt, where the Brotherhood came to power in the aftermath of protests in which the Brotherhood itself played a less pronounced role. Similarly in Tunisia, where the upheavals started, the Brotherhood-aligned Ennahda party made a bid for power, but only managed to gain power in a coalition with secular parties. In Syria, the Brotherhood also made a bid for power, but came up short faced with the Assad regime and its Iranian and Russian backers.

Perspectives on this rise of the Brotherhood differed greatly, even among Western commentators, and linked to a broader debate about the rise of Islamist movements across the region. Many observers warned of the anti-Western and anti-democratic ideology of the Brotherhood, and urged caution. Such observers essentially warned that while the regimes of Mubarak, Assad or Ben Ali were no angels, the rise of Islamist-oriented governments, however popular at the moment, would be no improvement. But this view ran up against a growing consensus that viewed the authoritarian regimes of the Middle East as the real challenge – and so-called "moderate" Islamists as part of the solution rather than a part of the problem. This debate had raged since the 1990s, and intensified following the September 11 attacks. It can be summarized in a simple question, "Why do they hate us?"

The answer, for many influential voices (including in the Bush Administration) was some combination of authoritarian government and poverty. Because America was viewed as the backer of authoritarian secular governments that failed to deliver economic development, Western observers feared that opposition to these governments was driven in the direction of underground Islamist movements. Because the more moderate among them were repressed, activists were pushed toward the more extremist underground movements. As a result, the answer to the problem was to reverse authoritarianism by supporting the democratization of the Middle East.

In reality, a massive amount of research has been done since 9/11 seeking to identify the drivers of radicalization and extremism, and has not been able to establish a clear link to authoritarian government. The body of research has pointed to many possible drivers of extremism, but neither authoritarian government nor poverty appear among the obvious answers. Yet following 9/11, many took such a link for granted. That was the key reason why Western leaders embraced "moderate Islamists" as a counterweight to the violent extremists of the Al Qaeda type, and leaned on governments to provide space of other forces, including Islamists, in the political system. Yet there was never a clear definition of who was a "moderate." To most Western observers, the answer was simply to define all groups that refrained from violence, irrespective of their ideology, as moderate. As we shall see, few Islamists saw this distinction as equally important as their Western interlocutors did.

Erdogan and the AKP in Turkey appeared ideal examples of moderate Islamists. Erdogan and his colleagues had broken away from the more austere Islamist party led by Necmettin Erbakan, and even declared their aspiration to guide Turkey into the EU. In its bid to unseat the tutelage of the Turkish military over politics, the AKP's rhetoric appealed not to Islamist ideology, but to democratic principles. Likewise, the small state of Qatar had welcomed dissidents from across the Middle East, and in 1996 launched a television station – Al Jazeera – that beamed across the Arab world by satellite, and provided a voice to many critics of authoritarian governments across the region. This positioned Qatar as an independent actor that built goodwill in circles critical of governments, particularly those close to the Brotherhood, whose leaders had been welcomed to the Emirate in the 1960s.

Meanwhile, across the region and among exiles in Europe, the Brotherhood itself grew considerably. Through a loose network of organizations that appeared independent from each other and often denied having any organic link with each other or even being part of the Brotherhood, the Muslim Brotherhood established social, intellectual and political organizations across the Arab world and beyond. Where permitted, it organized as a political party – the Islamic Action Front in Jordan, or under the name Al Islah (reform) in several other countries – or by electing individuals to parliament where it could not function as a party, as in Egypt or Kuwait. What, then, is the Brotherhood and what does it want?

The Brotherhood

The Muslim Brotherhood has done more than any other non-state organization to develop the ideology of political Islam and spread it across the world. It has the distinction of having impacted both the Salafi extremism of the Gulf, as well as its chief adversary – the millenarian extremism of Iran's revolutionaries.

And yet, there remains much confusion about the Brotherhood and its intentions.

The Muslim Brotherhood or *Ikhwan-al Muslimeen* was created in 1928 by Hassan al-Banna, the son of a Hanbali Sunni preacher in the Nile delta. He created the Brotherhood as a society that aimed to liberate the Muslim world from foreign domination, and to establish a unified Islamic state that would govern based on Islamic law and propagate the message of Islam to mankind. He saw violence as an entirely legitimate instrument for the spread of Islam.

Banna was motivated by Mustafa Kemal Atatürk's abolition of the Caliphate, which he saw as an unmitigated disaster. The end goal for the Brotherhood was the restoration of the Caliphate, but Banna saw it as a long-term goal that would be built from the bottom up, by indoctrinating individual Muslims who would band together to make society more Islamic, thus eventually enabling the takeover of political power and the recreation of a Caliphate.

What has made the Brotherhood successful is the creation of a hierarchical structure with concentric circles that fanned out across society. Brotherhood organizers and affiliates identify potential recruits that are socialized ever closer into the organization. Individuals have to progress over several steps to become full members, a socialization process that is carried out by "families" of several members that host recruits for recurrent meetings where Brotherhood ideology and loyalty is inculcated. In the first several steps, recruiters deny even being part of the organization. The formal incorporation into the Brotherhood is only done after a recruit has passed through several stages of indoctrination, ranging from supporters to affiliated to organizers before even becoming full "working brothers." This is one reason why the Brotherhood is such an amorphous network of affiliated groups – and why the leaders of so many Brotherhood-affiliated organizations claim, with a straight face, to have nothing to do with the Brotherhood. As the recruits close in on the inner circles, they are closely monitored by their superiors, who use elaborate forms to comment on the recruit's family, loyalty, knowledge of religion, and so forth.

Furthermore, for those within the inner circles, the Brotherhood promotes endogamy, in other words marriage across families of Brothers – thus increasing social control over recruits and reducing the risk of defections.[36] After all, if one's entire extended family is part of the Brotherhood network, defection becomes near-impossible. Under this pyramid-formed organization, Brotherhood members view themselves as an Islamic vanguard that is improving society, and organize within professional circles such as lawyers and doctors, thus building influence in society.

This, at least, is what happened in Egypt, with variations on the theme in other Arab countries. Each setting is different, as is the government attitude to the Brotherhood. This enabled the Brotherhood to expand in places like Jordan and Kuwait, and initially Saudi Arabia, where Brothers escaping repression in Egypt were welcomed to fill the need for educated professionals that the Kingdom itself could not produce. In other places like Syria and the UAE, the Brotherhood was repressed, leading to different local dynamics which affected the strategies pursued and whether

---

36   Sarah Ben Néfissa, "The Production of a "True Muslim" by the Egyptian Muslim Brotherhood: Loyalty and Dissent," *Revue internationale des Études du Développement*, no. 250, 2022.

the Brotherhood opted for political participation or more violent resistance.

It is often mentioned that Banna was inspired by Islamic reformers like Muhammad Abduh. However, crucially, Banna rejected their interest in modernizing the religion. Instead, he advocated the rejection of Western lifestyles and values and urged a return to the purity of early Islam. Most importantly, he saw Islam not just as a spiritual faith but as an all-encompassing system that governed everything from politics and economics to social questions and individual behavior. This led to the Brother-hood slogan "Islam is the solution." What this exactly meant was not clear, because Islamists hardly developed any concrete think-ing about what they meant with "Islam." Aside from backward-looking emphasis on following the Quran and Sunna, they never developed concrete thinking on how this would resolve problems of modern society or economics.

However, the political implications were clear: Banna opposed the notion of a multi-party system as "divisive," and instead advocated for the channeling of all political forces into a single Islamic front that would lead the nation to independence. This idea was eerily similar to the "democratic centralism" of Lenin and the Bolsheviks. And just as in the case of the Bolshe-viks, Banna did not reflect on how exactly an Islamic state would resolve all of the problems of the Muslim world. Like many Isla-mists, he appears to have figured that Islamic government would somehow automatically remove all ills from society.

Banna was no accomplished ideologue, but others would fill that void. The most important were Abu A'la Mawdudi and Sayyid Qutb. Mawdudi was born in 1903 in Aurangabad in India.

He would establish the Jamaat-i-Islami, which remains the primary Islamist organization in South Asia and is essentially analogous to the Muslim Brotherhood in ideology, although not in its organizational form. Mawdudi similarly saw the decline of Islam as a result of corruption by non-Islamic tendencies and urged a return to purity. A true millenarian, Mawdudi redefined the concept of jihad, which had previously mainly been seen as meaning defensive war, to legitimize a war that would enable Islam to take over the world. He also redefined the Islamic concept of *Jahiliya* (the age of ignorance) from meaning the pre-Islamic Arab society to signifying any place and time where an Islamic state has yet to be implemented. His argument was succinct: "Islam is a revolutionary ideology and programme which seeks to alter the social order of the whole world and rebuild it in conformity with its own tenets and ideals. … Islam wishes to destroy all States and Governments anywhere on the face of the earth which are opposed to the ideology and programme of Islam regardless of the country or the Nation which rules it."[37]

This was a radical innovation, and an indication that the Islamist ideology borrowed heavily from the tactics and methods of Europe's modern ideologues, communists and fascists – while cloaking their militancy in Islamic terms. It would come to have widespread influence on Islamist movements globally, and Mawdudi came to be counted as the perhaps most influential of Islamist thinkers, along with Egyptian Sayyid Qutb.

Qutb joined the Muslim Brotherhood only later in life but became its chief ideologue, and played a key role in driving the movement in a radical and violent direction. He built on Mawdu-

---

37   Abul A'la Maududi, *Jihad in Islam*, Beirut: Holy Quran Publishing House, 1980, p. 5. (http://www.muhammadanism.org/Terrorism/jihah_in_islam/jihad_in_islam.pdf)

di's ideas on *Jahiliyah*, and argued that present-day Muslim rulers were insufficiently pious. Taking a page from the Saudi Wahhabis, he declared true Islam to be essentially extinct. Accordingly, those who opposed the Islamist "vanguard" were not Muslims at all and could therefore be excommunicated through *Takfir* and killed. This was a major departure from Islamic precedent, which prohibits the killing of Muslims, and laid the ground for the various violent extremist groups in the Muslim world that excommunicate anyone they perceive as insufficiently Islamic.

Qutb was also largely responsible for integrating genocidal anti-Semitic ideas that Islamists borrowed from European fascism, superimposing it on the traditional Muslim antipathy toward Jews. Qutb devoted an entire book to the subject.[38] He injects into Islamist ideology the notion of a Jewish world conspiracy, blaming Jews for everything from atheistic materialism to the destruction of the family and urging for their complete annihilation.[39] As Bassam Tibi has argued, Qutb and his followers gave "antisemitism a religious imprint and aimed to make it look like an authentic part of traditional Islam, not an import from the West."[40]

The ideology of the Muslim Brotherhood, then, is not a resuscitation of ancient ideas, but a thoroughly modern phenomenon inspired by European totalitarian ideologies. It is obsessed

---

38   Sayyid Qutb, *Ma'rakatuna ma'a al-Yahud*, [Our Struggle with the Jews], in translation as *Past Trials and Present Tribulations: A Muslim Fundamentalist's View of the Jews*, Pergamon Press, 1987.

39   Matthias Küntzel, *Jihad and Jew-Hatred: Islamism, Nazism and the Roots of 9/11*, New York: Telos Press, 2007.

40   Bassam Tibi, *Islamism and Islam*, New Haven: Yale University Press, 2012, p. 57. Also Tibi, "From Sayyid Qutb to Hamas: The Middle East Conflict and the Islamization of Anti-Semitism", ISGAP Working Paper, 2010.

with political domination, differentiating Islamism from the traditional Islamic religion's focus on deliverance in the afterlife.

This ideology of the Muslim Brotherhood spread in many shapes and forms, and was by no means uniform. Qutb's extremism was mitigated to some extent by the efforts of Brotherhood leaders like Hasan al-Hudaybi, who preferred a more gradual and bottom-up approach of achieving the organization's results and opposed Qutb's emphasis on killing Muslim leaders. But these were disagreements over tactics, driven to a large degree by the fear of Hudaybi and those like him of government repression, rather than any disagreement about the desired end result.

The Rise of Political Islam in Turkey

Turkish political Islam has frequently been termed "moderate." This moderation, however, was very much a result of the political environment Islamists found themselves in, where a regime of military "tutelage" prevented Islamists from acceding to power and hindered their mobilization. Even when electorally successful, they had to contend with a judicial system stacked against them, and in the final analysis a military bureaucracy that saw Islamists as a dangerous counter-elite. The military had no problem with Islam, however. In the 1980s, the military itself sponsored the resurgence of Sunni Islam to counter left-wing mobilization – but it certainly was watchful of Islamist forces in society challenging the Turkish Kemalist system.

The Islamist movement grew in Turkish society, building on conservative opposition to Atatürk's secularizing reforms, and gained strength with the introduction of democracy in the 1950s.

This movement was inspired by two key ideological sources: the Naqshandi-Khalidi religious order, and the modern ideology of the Muslim Brotherhood. The Khalidi order, part of the broad Naqshbandiyya network, emerged in the nineteenth century as a focal point of resistance to the westernizing reforms in the late Ottoman Empire. The Khalidis urged for Islam to be the guideline for reform and for stricter application of Sharia law.[41] Their rise to prominence brought about a new force in Turkey's religious life. Whereas Turkey was overwhelmingly Hanafi and its Islamic scholars followed the more moderate Maturidi theology, the Khalidi order brought into Turkish Islam the more austere Shafi'i school of Islamic law and the stricter Ashari school of theology prevalent in the Arab Middle East.

The Khalidi Sheikh Mehmet Zahid Kotku, who headed the Iskenderpasha lodge of the Khalidi order in Istanbul, became the most important force that supported the emergence of Islamist politics in Turkey. Kotku encouraged a generation of pious Muslims to take positions in the state bureaucracy, and started the process of infiltration and takeover of state institutions that would help political Islam dominate Turkey. As Turkish scholar Birol Yeşilada noted, Kotku's followers worked to "conquer the state from within" by aligning themselves with powerful forces in business and politics.[42] It was Kotku who approved the creation of an Islamist political party, urging Necmettin Erbakan to split from Turkey's center-right in 1969. Tellingly, Recep Tayyip Erdogan himself was a member of the Iskenderpasha lodge.

---

41   Şerif Mardin, "The Nakshibendi Order of Turkey", *Fundamentalisms and the State*, ed. Martin E. Marty and R. Scott Appelby, Chicago: University of Chicago Press, 1993, p. 213.

42   Birol Yeşilada, "The Refah Party Phenomenon in Turkey," in Birol Yeşilada, ed. *Comparative Political Parties and Party Elites: Essays in Honor of Samuel J. Eldersveld*, Ann Arbor: University of Michigan Press, 1999, p. 137.

The second major influence on Turkish political Islam was the Muslim Brotherhood, whose ideology came to Turkey from the 1950s onward through the translation of key Brotherhood figures, including Qutb. The connections ran deep. Erbakan's 2011 funeral, tellingly, was attended by a who's who of the global Brotherhood movement. In presence were the Muslim Brotherhood's former spiritual guide, Mohamed Mahdi Akef, Hamas leader Khaled Meshaal, and Tunisian Islamist leader Rashid al-Ghannouchi.[43] The latter observed that in the Arab world of his generation, people talked about Erbakan in the same manner as they talked about Banna and Qutb.[44]

Erbakan was motivated by the same hatred toward Jews that the Brotherhood ideologues were. In his posthumously published memoir, he speaks of Jews as "a force that wants to ensure its hegemony and enslave, subordinate, and exploit all humans," and defines Judaism as "an ideology created by rabbis based on racial arrogance, and then decorated to look like a religion."[45]

This, then, is the ideological environment from which Erdogan and his closest associates emerged. Erdogan himself was influenced in particular by another Islamist ideologue, Necip Fazıl Kısakürek, who advocated for what one academic calls "the introduction of a totalitarian Islamist regime inspired by the Turkish-Islamist synthesis."[46]

---

43   "Global Muslim Brotherhood Leadership Gathers at Erbakan Funeral," *Global Muslim Brotherhood Daily Watch*, March 20, 2011, http://www.globalmbwatch.com/2011/03/20/global-muslim-brotherhood-leadership-gathers-at-erbakan-funeral/.

44   "Tunisian Islamist Leader Embraces Turkey, Praises Erbakan," *Hürriyet Daily News*, March 3, 2011.

45   Necmettin Erbakan, *Davam: Ne Yaptıysam Allah Rızası için Yaptım*, [My Struggle: whatever I did, I did for God's approval] Ankara: Milli Görüş Vakfı, 2011, p. 73.

46   Tunç Aybak, "The Sultan is Dead, Long Live 'Başyüce' Erdogan Sultan!," *Open Democracy*, May 31, 2017. (https://www.opendemocracy.net/tun-aybak/sultan-is-dead-long-live-ba-y-ce-erdogan-sultan.)

Erbakan managed to benefit from the decline of the Turkish center-right to come out with the largest vote in the 1995 parliamentary election, and formed a coalition government with a more secular party. Meanwhile, Erdogan won the mayoral election in Istanbul, a position that would catapult him to national office. But Erbakan's efforts to implement his Islamist agenda led the Turkish establishment to react, and he was ousted from power in 1997. This is what led Erdogan and his associates to break out from Erbakan's leadership and form a new party that appealed to a broader, centrist audience. Their timing could not have been better. At home, a devastating financial crisis opened a rare window for a new movement to take over the political system, and internationally Erdogan emerged on the scene exactly when the United States was searching for "moderate Islamists" who could form a counterweight to the violent extremists like Al Qaeda.

Qatar's Calculus

Qatar's rise as a force in Middle East politics has been one of the most remarkable facets of the past few decades. This small emirate the size of Connecticut had a population of only 50,000 in the early 1960s, but reached 1 million in 2006 and currently stands at 2.7 million people – of which the large majority are expatriates. This trend is not dissimilar from that of other Gulf emirates, most notably the UAE. Still, it is perhaps the most dramatic, given the sheer remoteness and poverty of the Qatar peninsula less than a lifetime ago.

Equally dramatic is the way in which Qatar emerged as a power-broker, intervening overtly as well as covertly in various conflicts across the region. It bucked the regional trend whereby the Gulf monarchies shunned revolutionary movements and instead sought to protect the regional status quo.

Qatar's ruling Emirs took a very different approach than their counterparts in the UAE. They long welcomed a variety of dissidents from across the Arab world, who set up shop in Qatar and were offered opportunities in media, academia, religious institutions and government. While this included Arab nationalists and other secular intellectuals, it most prominently featured Islamist groups from the Arab world and beyond, ranging from Al Qaeda-affiliated figures to the Afghan Taliban. Most prominent among these has been the Muslim Brotherhood.

The Brotherhood's links to Qatar go back to the early 1960s, when several prominent Brotherhood figures found refuge in the Emirate after their fortunes turned sour in Egypt. Most prominent among these was Yusuf al-Qaradawi, who had been jailed several times in Egypt in the 1940s and 50s. Qaradawi was welcomed by Qatari Emir Ali bin Abdullah al-Thani, who sympathized with the Brotherhood arrivals as persecuted pious Muslims. Qaradawi came to lead the establishment of Islamic studies in Qatar, becoming the founding dean of the Sharia Faculty at Qatar University when it was established in the 1970s. In Doha, the Brotherhood found a welcoming home, and a base from which they were able to spread their influence in the Gulf region. Notably, it was from Qatar that the Brotherhood worked to establish a base in the UAE.

The impact of the Brotherhood, and particularly Qaradawi's Friday sermons, grew exponentially after the Qatari Emir Sheikh Hamad bin Khalifa al-Thani created the Al Jazeera cable television network in 1996. Al Jazeera spread rapidly to become the most popular channel in the Arab world, and provided a platform for dissident voices that criticized other Arab regimes. Except Qatar, of course. And on Al Jazeera, Qaradawi had the opportunity to spread his ideology and thus that of the Brotherhood.

Qaradawi called himself a moderate, but his definition of the term is different than what Westerners define as moderate. He did distance himself from the likes of Al Qaeda and ISIS, decrying their indiscriminate killing and their indifference to the killings of other Muslims – advocating instead for the spread of Islamist ideology across the Muslim world and subsequently the rest of the world. But Qaradawi explicitly condoned not just violence but also suicide bombings when targeting an occupying force. More explicitly, he approved of suicide bombings against Israeli and Jewish targets around the world, under the pretext that any Jewish target is an Israeli target. He also approved of attacks on U.S. Forces in Iraq. He was a strong advocate of providing Muslims in the West with parallel legal systems – in anticipation of the emergence of a global Caliphate. Qaradawi in 2003 preached that Islam would return victorious to conquer Europe, this time not by the sword but through the spread of Islamist ideology through the continent.[47]

Both *Al Jazeera* and *Qaradawi* would play key roles in the Arab Upheavals of 2011. But they also created friction between Qatar and many Arab states, including Egypt and Saudi Arabia. In spite of this friction, the Qatari government continued backing the network. At times, they might order it to tone down its

---

[47] "Sheikh Yusuf al-Qaradawi and His Impact on the Dissemination of Radical Islam," Meir Amit Intelligence and Terrorism Information Center, 23 October 2022. (https://www.terrorism-info.org.il/en/sheikh-yusuf-al-qaradawi-and-his-impact-on-the-dissemination-of-radical-islam/)

rhetoric on a given issue, but kept building its reach as it branched out into new ventures, including channels in English and other languages.

This raises the question why Qatar took such a different route than other Gulf monarchies. Of course, sponsoring Islamic causes was hardly unique. As we have seen, following the Iranian revolution the Saudis did the same, seeking to spread their Salafism across the Muslim world and beyond. In the case of Qatar, many observers have similarly pointed to the opportunistic reasons for Doha to back the Muslim Brotherhood, as a vehicle among many to boost the Emirate's standing in regional and world politics – alongside its many business ventures like Qatar Airways, or its investment in sports, including organizing the 2022 World Cup of soccer. Advocates of this argument of Qatari pragmatism have noted that the country has simultaneously hosted a large U.S. air base since the early 2000s, and allowed an Israeli trade office to open in 1996, though it closed in 2000. And Qatar – like Ankara – long defended its relationships with extremist movements like Hamas or the Taliban by arguing that it provided its good offices as a useful intermediary for America and more broadly the West with movements that Western powers could not or did not want to talk to. When this became necessary, Doha's relations with them – and the fact that many of them lived in Qatar or kept offices there – became a boon to American interests, Doha argued. In other words, Qatar's outreach to extremist networks came to be sold as a positive rather than a negative.

There is much logic in this assessment. Further, the argument has been made that Qatar embraced the Brotherhood to further separate itself from Saudi Arabia, which it viewed as the chief threat to Qatari statehood. Still, Doha's strong ties with the Brotherhood betrays something deeper. First, the policy appears to have been animated by a wager (however mistaken) that the Brotherhood ideology would be a good horse to bet on in Middle East politics; and second, it would seem, an ideological affinity that the Al-Thani family (very much unlike their counterparts in Abu Dhabi) shared with the Brotherhood. The deference shown by the Qatari ruling family to the likes of Qaradawi, and their regular meetings over many years with representatives of the Brotherhood and its derivatives like Hamas and Ennahda would suggest an affinity that goes beyond just common interests.

Gulf politics are often very personal. Just as Abu Dhabi's distaste for the Brotherhood can be attributed in the final analysis largely to Mohammed bin Zayed's personal revulsion for the Brotherhood, so Qatar's support for it must be attributed to the sympathy Qatari rulers from Ali bin Abdullah to the present appear to have felt for the Brotherhood.

The AKP's Foreign Policy

Turkey's return to Middle East politics following the end of the Cold War was in many ways a function of the country's security situation and the perception of threats coming from the Middle East. Erdogan's AKP government, by contrast, toned down the threats coming from the region, and instead emphasized the opportunities. The ideological underpinnings of this initiative soon became clear – along with Turkey's efforts to establish influence in the region came its support for political Islam.

After Hamas came to power in Gaza in 2006, Turkey

wholeheartedly embraced this terrorist organization as legitimate freedom fighters – and showed a strong preference for Hamas over its more moderate Palestinian rivals in Fatah. This embrace of Hamas has been constant, as Erdogan even after the horrific pogrom of October 7, 2024, rejected classifying Hamas as a terrorist group. Erdogan also repeatedly ignored international concern over his closeness to Sudanese ruler Omar al-Bashir. He also promoted Ahmet Davutoglu, a previously obscure academic, as his main foreign policy advisor and later foreign minister. Davutoglu's writings provided ample notice of his ideological agenda: his 1992 book *Alternative Paradigms* was more or less a frontal attack on the Enlightenment values that form the base for Western society. In the book, he castigates the West for differentiating between reason and divine revelation, promoting instead the "unity of being and truth" expressed in Islam. He goes as far as to blame the Enlightenment for causing an "acute crisis" in Western civilization. Needless to say, Davutoglu states his opposition to the Kemalist aim of making Turkey a part of the West. By emphasizing its Islamic identity instead, Davutoglu argues that Turkey could establish its affinity with other Middle Eastern states and provide an alternate geostrategic vision to the nation-state model imposed on the region by the West.

Erdogan and Davutoglu saw their opportunity to do just that when the Arab upheavals hit in early 2011. Having marinated in Islamist thinking since their formative years, these Turkish leaders perceived the events as the collapse of the Western-led order imposed on the Middle East following the collapse of the Ottoman Empire. Indeed, a senior AKP official told this author even before the 2011 Arab Upheavals that the "monarchies of the Arab world" – in which he explicitly included Egypt – would soon fall, leading to the emergence of new regimes in the mold of the AKP.

Erdogan himself at times blasted the 1916 Sykes-Picot agreement, in which France and Britain divided up zones of influence in the Middle East – going so far as to accusing modern-day "Lawrences of Arabia" of interfering in regional matters. In this, Erdogan echoed the critique voiced by Islamist movements that consider the Western-imposed borders between Middle Eastern states – and in fact, these states themselves – to be artificial and illegitimate. And it led Turkey to emerge as a strong backer of the forces motivated by political Islam that challenged the *status quo* across the Middle East and North Africa.

This transformation of Turkish foreign policy from a stable, status quo-oriented policy to a radical approach that was perceived as subversive by several regional capitals reshuffled the politics of the region and led to serious concerns not just in the region but in the U.S. as well. Former National Security Advisor H.R. MacMaster in 2017 singled out Turkey and Qatar as the most significant supporters of radical Islamist ideology, and the next year, Mossad Chief Yossi Cohen reportedly called Turkey a potentially "even greater menace than Iran" in a meeting with intelligence chiefs of Egypt, Saudi Arabia and the UAE.

A Strange Axis Forms

As the Arab world went into multiple convulsions following the Arab Spring, a strange axis formed. In Turkey, Prime Minister Erdogan won re-election in summer 2011 and in his acceptance speech spoke as a representative of the whole Muslim world. "Beirut won as much as Izmir, Damascus won as much as Ankara,

Ramallah, Nablus, Jenin, the West Bank, Jerusalem won as much as Diyarbakir."[48]

Turkey emerged as the leading backer of the Muslim Brotherhood government in Egypt, as an early support of regime change in Syria, and as a direct participant in the conflict over government in Libya. It also put Turkey on collision course with both the Arab monarchies and Israel, who all supported the reigning *status quo* and strongly opposed the rise to prominence of Sunni political Islam across the region. Indeed, Turkey's growing involvement in the region, and its alignment with Qatar, created a new force in Middle Eastern geopolitics that was inherently radical, challenging the *status quo* in ways not dissimilar from the way Iran did – and thus helping generate a deep split within the Sunni Muslim world.

In this environment, Qatar emerged as Turkey's main ally. Acting often in coordination, Ankara and Doha lent political and financial support to the Brotherhood in Syria, Egypt, Libya, Tunisia, Yemen and Gaza. Meanwhile, they stood out in the Sunni world for their ambivalence toward Iran: while some apprehension toward Tehran's ambitions remained, they seemed to feel a certain connection as representatives of political Islam, just like the Iranian rulers.

As their activism drew opposition from the conservative Sunni monarchies, the two grew closer. And when the Arab upheavals tore apart the region from 2011 onward, Ankara and Doha would jump on the opportunity to gain influence across the Middle East and North Africa.

---

48   "Turkey election: Victorious Erdogan pledges 'consensus'," BBC, June 13, 2011. (https://www.bbc.com/news/world-europe-13744972)

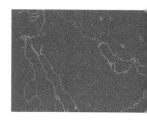

9.
THE ARAB UPHEAVALS: ISLAMISTS ADVANCE

In late 2010, protests began in Tunisia and spread across the Arab world. These protests were the result of a gradual buildup of frustration with the mismanagement and corruption of most Arab states, and with the political stagnation of the entire region. Many countries had been led by the same ruler for decades. Tunisian leader Zine el Abidin Ben Ali had been in power for twenty-four years; Hosni Mubarak in Egypt for thirty; and Libya's Moammar Qaddafi for a full forty-two years. Syria's Bashar al-Assad had only been in power for eleven years, but his father had ruled the country for twenty-nine years before him.

The revolts were caused by a multitude of factors including the rapidly changing societies of the Arab world, with their young and rapidly urbanizing population, exacerbated by the rise of food prices and the cost of living more generally. New communications technologies only accelerated the process.

Islamists were not initially at the forefront of the Arab

Upheavals, with the exception of Libya. In some countries, they at first did not even participate in the protests – in Egypt, the Brotherhood did so only after strong pressure from its younger ranks. This should not come as a surprise: these protests were spreading largely spontaneously, did not have clear leaders or organization, and no obvious agenda aside from the removal of authoritarian regimes and their mismanagement and corruption. Islamist groups had not planned these protests, and they did not necessarily fit with the Islamist agenda. In fact, most of the protestors, at least initially, appeared to be younger people whose appearance and demands had little to do with Islamic causes.

But once the immediate protests had subsided, Islamist movements turned out to be the force with the greatest where-withal to step into the void left by long-standing regimes. And they were not alone. Turkey and Qatar stepped in forcefully to support the Islamist forces that sought to use the opportunity to grab power. Qatar provided financial support by the barrel, whereas Turkey promoted its own model of an Islamist force able to come to power through elections and to steer the country in an Islamic direction. Of course, Erdogan and his associates did not mention that they were rapidly asserting control over the country through means that were themselves increasingly authoritarian.

Tunisia: The Beginnings

As protests gripped Tunisia in December 2010, Qatar's *Al Jazeera* network provided intensive coverage of the events in the country. Not staying at that, Al Jazeera's reporter in Tunisia became what a story from *The New York Times* called a "partisan" of the protests, actively helping disseminate cellphone videos of demonstrators and sporting an editorial line that was activist rather than journalistic. The protests succeeded in forcing the resignation of long-time leader Ben Ali, and two weeks after Ben Ali left for Saudi Arabia, Rashid Al-Ghannouchi, the leader of the Islamist Ennahda party, returned to Tunisia to lead the party as the country prepared for elections.

Ennahda, an offshoot of the Muslim Brotherhood, ran a well-oiled and obviously well-funded campaign. Its opponents quickly pointed to Qatar as the likely funder of the extravagant campaign, which featured the distribution of gifts of various types by Ennahda-related groups to the electorate. There was no blatant evidence, and Ennahda itself – rather unconvincingly – referred to the support of its members and some additional unspecified donations from Tunisian businessmen.

Ennahda managed to win 37 percent of the vote in the 2011 elections, allowing it to be the senior partner in a coalition government. The Qatar connections were immediately visible, as both the foreign minister and the minister for youth and sports in the government were Ennahda members who had worked in various capacities for Al Jazeera in Qatar.[49] Doha immediately pledged a $1 billion loan to Tunisia, helped shore up its central bank's position, promised several additional billions in investments and created programs to support employment prospects for Tunisian unemployed youth. Qatar rapidly became the largest Arab investor in Tunisia and second only to France in terms of its financial commitment.

Turkish involvement was less visible at first, but it served as

---

49   Julie Schneider, "Tunisie : d'où vient l'argent d'Ennahda?" *Le Point*, February 10, 2012. \

the role model for Ghannouchi and Ennahda. While Ghannouchi's opponents compared him to Khomeini, who similarly had
returned from exile abroad, Ghannouchi showed political acumen
by pointing instead to the democratically elected Erdoğan as his
inspiration and model. Ghannouchi was known to have championed a gradualist approach to taking power in Tunisia. He had
learnt from the Algerian experience, where Islamists had been
crushed by the army following an electoral victory three decades
earlier. Ghannouchi instead hoped, like Erdogan, to be able to
gain power by electoral means and then stay on to guide Tunisia
in an Islamist direction.

Once Ennahda was ensconced in power, Turkey's support
became more apparent. Ankara signed a Treaty on Friendship
and Cooperation in 2011, followed the next year by a High-Level
Strategic Cooperation Council for security and defense issues.
Turkish attention to Tunisia was nevertheless rather limited, not
least because it focused its attention on prizes that were both
much closer and much bigger – Syria and Egypt.

Egypt: Rise of the Brotherhood

When large-scale protests built against Egyptian leader Hosni
Mubarak in January 2011, Turkey and Qatar emerged as cheerleaders for change. Al Jazeera further amplified its role compared
to the coverage of Tunisian events. The channel dropped all its
scheduled programming and provided 24-hour coverage of the
Egyptian protests, and took on an overt role as cheerleader of
revolution with no pretense of balanced journalistic coverage.
The Egyptian regime's decision to ban the network only drove

Al Jazeera in an even more partisan direction. This editorial line led it to become a darling of the protesters, some of whom began waving Al Jazeera flags. More importantly, it helped set the tone across the Arab world and beyond, providing enthusiastic coverage of the revolutionaries and contributing to turning world opinion decisively in favor of the demonstrators.[50]

While Turkey had been more circumspect with regard to Tunisia, it took an active role when the protests hit Egypt. Within a week of the protests, Erdoğan issued what he termed a "candid warning" to Mubarak to "meet the people's desire for change." This was a major shift for Erdoğan, who had refused to comment on the massive protests against the Iranian regime less than two years earlier, or on the Mullah's brutal crackdown on the "Green revolution" and the large-scale protests that began in 2022. In the case of Egypt's secular regime, clearly, other standards applied.

In response to Mubarak's announcement that he would remain until the end of his term in September that year but not seek re-election, Erdoğan was the first foreign leader to call for Mubarak's resignation. While the Obama Administration contented itself with urging Mubarak to ensure that "change must begin now," Erdoğan called for Mubarak to give up power to a temporary administration.[51]

The Muslim Brotherhood, meanwhile, had come around to support the revolution. But this was not initially obvious. The demise of the regime would seem to be in line with the move-

50   Alia Nabil Eshaq, "Regional media and its role in Tahrir's revolution: Comparison between Al-Jazeera and Al-Arabiya," AUC Knowledge Fountain, 2011. (https://fount.aucegypt.edu/cgi/viewcontent.cgi?article=1025&context=studenttxt)

51   Thomas Seibert, "Turkey's Erdogan Says Mubarak Should Go Now," *The National*, February 3, 2011. (https://www.thenationalnews.com/world/mena/turkey-s-erdogan-says-mubarak-should-go-now-1.413650)

ment's interests. But the Brotherhood was split on the issue, not least since the regime's weakness had played in its favor. The older generation that led the Brotherhood continued to believe the movement must tread carefully in political matters, while advancing its position by its parallel emphasis on missionary, educational and social work. Before it deemed Egyptian society ready to embrace an Islamic state based on Sharia law, it feared that a premature attempt to take over the state would backfire – again, just as it had done in Algeria. By contrast, a weakened Mubarak regime would be forced to make concessions to the movement, many Brotherhood leaders thought.[52]

These views would prove prescient. But they were unable to hold in view of a younger, more politicized generation of Brotherhood activists, when confronted with the rapidly rising likelihood that the regime would indeed collapse. A few days into the protests, the Brotherhood joined in, but was careful to remain in the background. Still, the Brotherhood's decision to join the protests was key in tipping the balance in favor of the revolutionaries and dooming the Mubarak regime.

In the period of transition that followed Mubarak's resignation, Qatar and Turkey did not remain idle. Doha stepped in to help Egypt manage the economic fallout of the revolution, providing a gift of $500 million to stabilize the country's budget.[53] Ankara, meanwhile, was planning big. Turkish foreign minister Ahmet Davutoğlu, an Islamist ideologue himself and architect of Turkey's Islamist foreign policy, was a frequent visitor to Egypt, paving the way for Erdoğan to visit triumphally in September

---

52   Israel Elad-Altman, "The Egyptian Muslim Brotherhood After the 2005 Elections," *Current Trends in Islamist Ideology*, Nov. 1, 2006.

53   "Egypt Says Will Not Need IMF, World Bank Funds," Reuters, June 25, 2011.

2011. In the aftermath of the visit, Davutoğlu told the New York Times that "Egypt would become the focus of Turkish efforts, as an older American-backed order, buttressed by Israel, Saudi Arabia and, to a lesser extent, prerevolutionary Egypt, begins to crumble." Ankara's ambition, he said, was to "create a new axis of power at a time when American influence in the Middle East seems to be diminishing" to connect "the two biggest nations in our region, from the north to the south, from the Black Sea down to the Nile Valley in Sudan."[54]

In months that followed, the domestic balance in Egypt shifted radically in favor of the Brotherhood axis. In parliamentary elections in December 2011 and January 2012, the Brotherhood's Justice and Freedom Party gained half of the parliamentary seats, and the Salafist Nur party another quarter of the seats. Over 65 percent of Egyptians had voted for one of the two Islamist groups. If the Tahrir square protests had been dominated by urban youths and Islamists only formed a limited part, in the population at large the Islamist parties showed their superior level of organization and support. In May-June 2012, Brotherhood candidate Muhammed Morsi won the presidency in a narrow 51.7 percent victory over former Egyptian Air Force chief Ahmed Shafik.

Those elections showed the power of the Islamist movement, but also the strong opposition to it among considerable portions of the Egyptian electorate. Turkey and Qatar now moved in to help the Brotherhood consolidate power. While financial power, unlike Gulf monarchies, was never Turkey's forte, Ankara in September 2012 announced a $2 billion loan to support the Egyp-

---

54   Anthony Shadid, "Turkey Predicts Alliance with Egypt as Regional Anchors," *New York Times*, September 18, 2011.

tian economy.[55] Doha stepped in with more financial muscle. In August, the Emirate had announced its own $2 billion deposit into the Egyptian central bank during Emir Hamad's visit to Cairo to meet Morsi, and the following month it announced plans to invest $18 billion into industry and tourism projects to help develop the Egyptian economy. Qatar also acted as the interlocutor between the Brotherhood and the United States during Morsi's rise to power.[56]

Soon after assuming power, Morsi made a trip to Turkey as a guest of honor at the AK Party convention, alongside Hamas leader Khaled Mesha'al. In November 2012, Erdoğan was in Cairo to sign thirty-odd agreements to deepen bilateral cooperation. Qatari and Turkish support appear to have emboldened the Brotherhood to assert control over Egypt. In fall 2012, Morsi dismissed military leaders that had served as a check on his power. He then sought to rush the work of a constitutional assembly tasked to draft a new constitution. When liberal and minority representatives boycotted the work, claiming the Islamists were using the Assembly to dictate the drafting of the new constitution, Morsi in November 2012 issued a decree that granted himself sweeping executive and legislative powers and exempted his actions from judicial review.

This move kickstarted public protests against him, which eventually would end his time in power several months later. But Erdogan was unperturbed. In December, after Morsi rammed the new constitution through a referendum with a low turnout of 32 percent, Erdoğan called to congratulate him, and termed

55   "Turkey to Provide Egypt $2 Billion in Aid," *Wall Street Journal*, September 15, 2012.

56   Lina Khatib, "Qatar and the Recalibration of Power in the Gulf," Carnegie Middle East Center, September 2014. (https://carnegieendowment.org/files/qatar_recalibration.pdf)

the new document an important step for Egypt's stability.[57] There is little doubt Erdoğan saw it as a step in the consolidation of Brotherhood control over Egypt and thus of the dominance of the Brotherhood axis over the Middle East. As we will see, however, it was the beginning of the end.

During his time in power, Morsi also cautiously opened up relations with Iran, becoming the first Egyptian leader in 30 years to visit Tehran. In spite of the ideological affinity between the Iranian regime and the Brotherhood, the opening was relatively guarded. Egypt's military and security structures remained wary of Tehran, and the Iranian support for the Assad regime in Syria temporarily raised sectarian divides between Brotherhood supporters and Tehran.

Libya: Jostling Begins

Very soon after the Tunisian protests began, unrest spread to neighboring Libya. The unrest swelled particularly in the eastern port city of Benghazi, where the opposition took control in late February. Moammar Gaddafi's violent repression of protests triggered a perception of a humanitarian emergency both in Western capitals and some Arab quarters. Qatar, which at the time held the presidency of the Arab League, jumped on the opportunity to intervene. Doha took the lead in having the Arab League pass a resolution demanding a no-fly zone in Libya and calling for a military intervention. The Organization of Islamic Cooperation, chaired by Turkish Egyptian-born Islamic scholar Ekmeleddin Ihsanoğlu, did the same.

---

57   "Erdogan Pays Congratulatory Call to Morsi", *Daily Sabah*, December 24, 2012.

When NATO stepped in to impose a no-fly zone, Qatar and the UAE sent fighter jets to participate, ensuring the operation did not come to be seen as another purely Western intervention in a Muslim country. While the two Gulf states were initially aligned, they would soon plunge into a deep rivalry over Libya.

Qatar took a decisive role in supporting the Libyan rebel government based in Benghazi. It was among the first states to grant it diplomatic recognition. It also provided arms, trained rebel fighters, and sent Qatari military units to support the rebels. Not staying at that, Qatar used its financial muscle in support of the insurgency. It helped the rebel government market oil products on world markets, and bailed it out when it had difficulty engaging in international financial transactions.[58]

Yet Qatari support was very selective. In a pattern that would be repeated in Syria, Qatar focused its support on specific Islamist groups, and particularly those connected with the Muslim Brotherhood. This includes Brotherhood-linked militias in the Benghazi area, but also Salafi-Jihadi militias connected with the Libyan Islamic Fighting Group. This outfit, based on Libyan fighters in the Afghan war against the Soviet occupation, had well-documented links to Al Qaeda and was listed as a terrorist group in the United Kingdom.[59]

This preference for Islamists ruffled feathers. Time Magazine in January 2012 cited high-level figures in the National Transitional Council complaining that Qatar's assistance empowered a "narrow clique of Islamists," in order to "basically support the

---

58   Guido Steinberg, "Qatar and the Arab Spring," SWP Comments, February 2012. (https://www.swp-berlin.org/publications/products/comments/2012C07_sbg.pdf)

59   Sudarsan Raghavan, "These Libyans were once linked to al-Qaeda. Now they are politicians and businessmen," *Washington Post*, September 28, 2017.

Muslim Brotherhood."[60] Over time, this led to growing criticism of Qatar, and may in a sense have backfired. The Brotherhood's Justice and Construction Party – its name a near-carbon copy of Erdoğan's Justice and Development Party – obtained about 10 percent of the vote in elections in July 2012, still coming in in second place.

As for Turkey, its role was initially more ambiguous, not least because of Turkey's large investments in Libya and the presence of hundreds of Turkish nationals in the country. This led Ankara to initially take a cautious approach. Erdoğan came out against a NATO intervention in March 2011, but had to backtrack within ten days. In fact, later many in Turkey concluded this late response had undermined Turkish abilities to influence the course of events in the Libyan transition, in turn influencing Turkish decision-making on Syria. In any case, Turkey soon joined the Qatari approach to Libya, and called for Gaddafi's removal. In July, Turkish Foreign Minister Ahmet Davutoğlu visited Benghazi, and Ankara committed several hundred million dollars in aid to the NTC. In September 2011 – even before Gaddafi was killed by a mob in the coastal city of Sirte, Erdoğan visited Tripoli and received a hero's welcome. As will be seen in the next chapter, however, Turkey's major bid for influence in Libya would come several years later during the second Libyan civil war, when it would intervene to stop the forces aligned with the UAE and Egypt from gaining control of the country.

---

60   Steven Sotloff, "Why the Libyans Have Fallen Out of Love with Qatar," *Time*, January 2, 2012.

The Syrian Quagmire

The Syrian civil war has been both the most deadly and the most convoluted of the proxy conflicts of the Middle East in the past decade. Much like Afghanistan in the 1990s, the internal conflict rapidly got overtaken by the competing interests of almost every regional and great power involved in Middle Eastern affairs. While Libya and Egypt turned mainly into struggles within the Sunni world, Syria became a trilateral affair involving the Brotherhood Axis, the Arab *status quo* powers, as well as Iran. As is clear today, Iran and Russia came out on top in this struggle, by succeeding in helping the Assad regime survive what sometimes appeared an impossible struggle. This outcome, in turn, was possible – aside from the decisive Iranian support – largely because of the infighting among the Sunni powers. Particularly following the Muslim Brotherhood victory in Egypt, the specter of a regional takeover by the Islamist group led to a split among the powers seeking Assad's overthrow.

In the early days of the Arab Upheavals, however, things looked very different. When the uprising against the Assad regime began, most Sunni powers had invested considerable energy in building relations with Damascus, in an effort to reduce Iranian influence over the regime. From Turkey to Qatar and Saudi Arabia, the Sunni powers at first urged Assad to reform the system and make it more inclusive. Erdoğan had spent the better part of a decade courting the Assad family, viewing Syria as the key country – a gateway of sorts – to expand Turkish influence across the Arab world. As the uprising grew, Turkish leaders expected their new-won influence to help them alter the behavior of the Assad regime, which by spring and summer of

2011 was viciously cracking down on protests. Ankara urged Assad to include opposition forces and particularly the Muslim Brotherhood in the country's political system. Indeed, Erdoğan had never sought to hide his affinity for the Brotherhood in his interactions with Assad, repeatedly asking him to legalize the group and seeking to mediate between Assad and the Syrian *Ikhwan*.[61] But Turkish demands fell on deaf ears, the Brotherhood joined the armed opposition to Assad, and by November 2011 Turkey officially called for Assad's removal and began supporting the opposition.

A multitude of rebel groups emerged in Syria, but most aside from the Kurdish forces in the northeast had one thing in common: they were based on Sunni Arab identity politics. This does not mean that one should accept the simplistic notion of a Sunni-Shia conflict with the Alawites in the Shi'a camp. It is true that Syria is a mirror image of Iraq: two thirds of the population consists of Sunni Arabs, but Alawites, who form ten percent of the population, are heavily overrepresented in the government and security forces. Still, the regime is not just an Alawite regime: it spent great efforts to include particularly urban merchant Sunnis into its power base. Two thirds of the Syrian army consists of Sunnis, and many leading regime posts are held by Sunnis.[62]

The notion of a sectarian conflict was thus one that was endorsed primarily by the Sunni Islamist opposition, which sought to mobilize both internally and externally around the objective of

61   "The Muslim Brotherhood in Syria," Carnegie Middle East Center, n.d. (https://carnegie-mec.org/syriaincrisis/?fa=48370&lang=en)

62   Chris Zambelis, "Syria's Sunnis and the Regime's Resilience," CTC Sentinel, vol. 8 no 5, 2015 (https://ctc.westpoint.edu/syrias-sunnis-and-the-regimes-resilience/); Cyrus Malik, "Washington's Sunni Myth and The Civil Wars In Syria And Iraq," *War on the Rocks*, August 16, 2016. (https://warontherocks.com/2016/08/washingtons-sunni-myth-and-the-civil-wars-in-syria-and-iraq/)

overthrowing an infidel regime. It was also endorsed by the Shi'a clerical regime in Iran, which sought to mobilize Shi'a militias to sustain the Syrian regime. The notion of a sectarian conflict was also largely internalized in the West, where it seemingly provided a logic to the madness of the Middle Eastern conflicts.

Syria's minorities – whether Alawite, Christians or Druze – did rally around the authoritarian but secular Assad regime, which they saw as a lesser evil than the likely alternative: a Sunni Islamist state, or perhaps Caliphate, where they would at best be relegated to second-class citizen status. But many urban, moderate or secularized Sunnis did exactly the same, since they had no desire to live in a Sunni theocracy either.

That being said, several different ideological categories emerged among the Sunni-based rebel forces: Salafi-Jihadi, broadly Islamist, Brotherhood-affiliated and secular-leaning opposition groups. These ideological lines were often blurred by cross-cutting tribal, financial or political links, making it difficult to discern the dividing lines among the fractious rebel groups. But it was clear from the start that the outside powers bet on different horses in this race. Western powers found themselves, perhaps unexpectedly, aligned with the Saudi and Emirati governments in supporting the more secular and gradualist elements of the opposition – groups that sought to reform rather than raze the existing state institutions in Syria.

They did so for different reasons. Western powers largely subscribed to the notion of a broad-based government for Syria's future, which would provide a voice to all groups within Syrian society, and would prove acceptable to the non-Sunni constituencies that the Assad regime depended on for its support base. Saudi and Emirati rulers, by contrast, came to see the rise of political Islam across the Middle East as a threat to their own security. In this, they were concerned both with the Muslim Brotherhood and with the Salafi-Jihadi ideology that had emerged as a cross-pollination of the most virulent strains of Brotherhood ideology with Salafi theology. As we have seen, while Salafis had tradition-ally been "quietist" in the sense of remaining loyal to monarchical regimes, Qutb's ideas had helped generate a more activist, some-times fanatic offshoot of Salafism that developed into the *Sahwa* movement in Saudi Arabia, and which degenerated into jihadi groups like Al Qaeda.

Thus, conservative Gulf regimes were torn. On one hand, they viewed the uprising in Syria as a possible blow to Iranian interests in the region, and supported the notion of a Syria run by members of its Sunni Arab majority. But on the other hand, they feared that a victory of political Islam in Syria would spread across the region and jeopardize their own domestic security. Thus the UAE remained largely aloof from the conflict, and the Saudis got involved mainly to ensure that groups aligned with its domestic enemies did not gain the upper hand.

Turkey and Qatar had no such inhibitions. Quite to the contrary, they embraced the Islamist elements of the opposition and particularly the Brotherhood forces. Their urge to support the armed revolt was also affected by the rapid demise of the Qaddafi regime in Libya, which had taken them by surprise. In Syria, they anticipated a rapid fall of the Assad regime and placed their bets on supporting a Brotherhood-led regime that would replace it. The Syrian National Council, a Brotherhood-dominated body that Doha and Ankara supported, would step in and take power.[63] But Brotherhood efforts to dominate the opposition faced opposition not least because the Syrian Brotherhood had been decimated by Assad's father in the 1980s, when it viciously repressed a Brotherhood uprising, culminating in the 1982 Hama massacre. The *Ikhwan* was outlawed, which made it unable to develop the type of support in society that it enjoyed in Egypt.

By late 2012, the U.S. strongarmed Qatar into hosting a conclave to unite the Syrian opposition, a National Coalition, that would be more open to non-Brotherhood forces. But even here, the Brotherhood remained the most organized and ambitious group.[64] Turkish-American differences also emerged on what rebel groups to support.

The Turks and Qataris gravely underestimated the resilience and staying power of the Assad regime. When they realized the Brotherhood simply lacked the wherewithal to topple Assad, their solution was not to embrace a broader, more unified opposition – they did the opposite. Instead, Turkey and Qatar facilitated the rise of more extremist armed groups. One of these was Ahrar al-Sham, a group in northwest Syria that combined Salafi and Brotherhood lineages.[65] Another was the Nusra Front, an Al Qaeda affiliate in Syria that became the destination of numerous foreign fighters that flooded into Syria. During this period, Qatar liberally funded Islamist groups that fought the Assad regime, whereas Turkey at times looked the other way, and other times

63   Michael Stephens, "Where Did it All Go Wrong? The Qatar-Turkey Power House Comes Up Short," Royal United Services Institute, January 14, 2014.

64   Rania El Gamal and Andrew Hammond, "Mistrust of Syria's Muslim Brotherhood Lingers," Reuters, November 13, 2012. (https://reuters.com/article/syria-crisis-brotherhood-idUSL5E8MCAPZ20121112/)

65   Anand Gopal and Jeremy Hodge, "Social Networks, Class, and the Syrian Proxy War," New America, April 2021, p. 29. (https://www.jstor.org/stable/pdf/resrep30592.7.pdf)

actively facilitated the flow of foreign fighters across its porous border with Syria.[66] Both powers actively helped arm the Islamist fighters seeking to overthrow Assad.

In doing so, however, they played into Assad's hands. Assad's regime had long concluded that to survive, it needed to engineer a situation where outside forces faced a binary choice between the regime and Sunni jihadi terrorists. In this, Assad took a page from the Russian playbook. Faced with an insurgency in Chechnya, Moscow in the 1990s painted itself as a misunderstood defender of Europe against the threat of Islamic radicalism. But from 1999 onwards, Moscow targeted almost exclusively the nationalist Chechen leadership that happened to enjoy international support, while leaving the jihadi elements within the insurgency alone. As a result, the nationalist insurgency gradually got decimated, the jihadis grew, and Moscow was able to portray the struggle as one between its own henchmen in Chechnya and the terrorists.

From the start, Assad had similarly claimed that all opposition to his regime consisted of terrorists. He proceeded to make sure this happened, by systematically facilitating the rise of the Islamic State terrorist group. Damascus had long-standing connections to the group, which it had deployed in Iraq against the U.S. occupation, and who enjoyed preferential treatment in Syria's Sednaya prison. Assad proceeded to release hundreds of Jihadists from prison, while actively facilitating the rise of ISIS in several ways. The regime neglected to target the group while it bombed the strongholds of the less radical rebel groups. It also bought oil from ISIS-controlled areas, generating income for the

---

66   Bipartisan Policy Center, "Turkey: An Increasingly Undependable Ally," April 2015. (https://
      bipartisanpolicy.org/download/?file=/wp-content/uploads/2019/03/BPC-Turkey-Alliance.pdf)

group, and at times appeared to coordinate its actions with ISIS detachments.[67]

Assad also dealt Ankara another massive blow. When Turkey began supporting the rebel forces, Assad simply handed over control of large areas of northern Syria to Turkey's arch-enemy, the Kurdish terrorist PKK organization and its Syrian affiliate, the PYD.[68]

In this way, Assad managed to change the priorities for key adversaries. The creation of a PKK-controlled statelet in northern Syria suddenly changed Ankara's priorities from offensive to defensive – making the struggle against Kurdish separatism a priority over support for Syrian regime change. Meanwhile, the rise of ISIS shifted American priorities, with the goal of ensuring Assad's demise distinctly taking a back seat to fighting the Sunni jihadism of Islamic State.

Paving the Way for the Sunni Civil War

Through their actions in Tunisia, Libya, Egypt and Syria, Turkey and Qatar helped generate a civil war of sorts within the Sunni orbit. Their dogged determination to advance the position of political Islam and particularly the Muslim Brotherhood in the countries affected by the Arab Upheavals triggered a reaction. This reaction was twofold: internal as well as regional. In the region, the conservative monarchies – particularly Saudi Arabia and the

---

67   Matthew Levitt, "The Role of the Islamic State in the Assad Regime's Strategy for Regime Survival: How and Why the Assad Regime Supported the Islamic State," in Christiane Höhn, Isabel Saavedra, and Anne Weyembergh, *The Fight against Terrorism: Achievements and Challenges - Liber Amicorum Gilles de Kerchove*, Larcier Intersentia, 2021. (https://www.washingtoninstitute.org/media/4698)

68   Jordi Tejel, "Syria's Kurds: Troubled Past, Uncertain Future," Carnegie Endowment for International Peace, October 16, 2012. (https://carnegieendowment.org/2012/10/16/syria-s-kurds-troubled-past-uncertain-future-pub-49703)

UAE – proved increasingly determined to stop and reverse the Brotherhood's momentum. But equally important was the internal aspect. Leaders in Doha and Ankara, blinded by their own ideological perspectives, viewed the Brotherhood and Islamism as the dominant ideological and political force in the region's future. In this conviction they underestimated the resistance to the Brotherhood and to Islamism across the Arab world. Therefore, the Islamists supported by Doha and Ankara overreached. While possessing superior organization and motivation, they were also distrusted and feared by large swathes of society. In Tunisia, the secular opposition managed to check Ennahda's quest for power. In Libya, the Brotherhood's overreach triggered a strong reaction. In Egypt, Morsi's power grab kickstarted the path that ended in a military intervention. And in Syria, the ever more radical Islamist nature of the revolt helped solidify Assad's base.

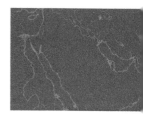

10.
THE SUNNI CIVIL WAR, 2013-20

The rise of the Brotherhood Axis in 2011-12 sent shockwaves around the Middle East and beyond. In the West, as noted, there was confusion as to what this meant. Initial jubilation over the impending democratic breakthrough in the Middle East gradually gave way to concerns over the intentions of the Islamist forces, as well as despair over the widespread violence in places like Syria and Libya. There was also a double backlash. The first was internal to the countries concerned. In Tunisia, civil society mobilized against the Ennahda party's efforts to insert Islamist priorities into the revamped constitution, and its coalition partners made it a priority to exclude Islamists from the Ministry of Education portfolio. In Libya and Egypt, the popular backlash to the Brotherhood's attempt to grab power mounted rapidly. Externally, meanwhile, the initial shock of the upheavals gave way to a determination among the opponents of the Brotherhood Axis to contain and rollback the spread of political Islam. This triggered a civil war in the Sunni Muslim world, which threatened to spread far out from the Middle East.

The Battle for Egypt

By late 2012, the Saudis and Qataris had begun to sharply differentiate the networks they funded in Syria, and in turn the factions of the Syrian opposition adjusted to this reality. In the end, the divide would turn out to benefit Iran and the Assad regime more than anyone else, certainly following the rise of ISIS. Meanwhile, Mohammed Morsi's power grab in Egypt during November and December seemed to confirm the suspicions among the opponents of political Islam that the Brotherhood would not forsake the opportunity of clinging to power.

In April 2013, a group of activists began collecting signatures for a massive protest on the first anniversary of Morsi's rule, which fell on June 30. The movement, known as *Tamarod* or "rebellion," rapidly gained support from numerous non-Islamist political parties and social movements. These protests, which grew to number in the millions on June 30 and subsequent days, led to deadly clashes with pro-Brotherhood groups, and eventually to the military intervention of July 3. Morsi and the Brotherhood leadership was arrested, and the Head of the Supreme Court appointed interim president.

There were, from the start, suspicions that the process leading to the ouster of Morsi had not been entirely "organic." In 2015, recordings were released that appeared to indicate that the Egyptian military had been intimately involved in the planning of the anti-Morsi demonstrations. Moreover, these recordings suggested that the UAE had contributed considerable financing to the effort to oust Morsi.[69] These recordings were rapidly slammed as fabricated by official Cairo, but are widely considered genuine.[70] Egyptian politicians have also accused Saudi Arabia of being involved in the planning of the military intervention.[71]

Indications of an Emirati and Saudi role are not exactly undermined by the speed with which Abu Dhabi and Riyadh stepped in to support the post-Brotherhood Egyptian government politically as well as financially. Within days of the military intervention, they had pledged over $12 billion in support for Egypt, a number that has been multiplied since then.[72] The Saudis and Emiratis treated the military intervention as a major victory in regional politics.

Qatar and Turkey were less pleased. Qatar's reaction was relatively muted, in great part because the Egyptian crisis occurred just as Qatar's Emir Hamad bin Khalifa al-Thani abdicated in favor of his son Tamim bin Hamad. This transition, apparently long since planned, allowed the 61-year old monarch to hand over power to his son while still able to help him consolidate power. It also meant a change in the style of Qatari diplomacy, as the younger al-Thani appeared to have a more cautious approach in regional affairs, following the extremely high profile his father had displayed in the previous decade. Emir Tamim sent a muted letter of congratulations to the interim President in Egypt, but

69   David D. Kirkpatrick, "Recordings Suggest Emirates and Egyptian Military Pushed Ousting of Morsi," *The New York Times*, March 1, 2015.

70   David D. Kirkpatrick, "Leaks Gain Credibility and Potential to Embarrass Egypt's Leaders". *The New York Times*. May 12, 2015.

71   "Ayman Nour: Saudi planned the coup in Egypt, UAE carried it out," *Middle East Monitor*, August 23, 2018.

72   Jeremy Ravinsky, "Friends again? Saudi Arabia, UAE jump in to aid Egypt," *Christian Science Monitor,* July 10, 2013.

welcomed Brotherhood exiles that now flooded out of Egypt, indicating the change in Qatar was one of style more than substance.

Turkey's reaction was less subdued. Prime Minister Erdogan strongly condemned the Egyptian coup, terming its perpetrators "state terrorists" and "brutal murderers." He equated Al-Sisi with Syria's Assad, and lashed out at Western powers that did not, in his view, sufficiently condemn the coup – and had choice words also for the Gulf states that moved in to support the post-Morsi government. As Erdogan pulled Turkey's ambassador from Cairo, a major blow had been dealt to Turkey's project of change in the Middle East. Ankara suddenly found itself moving from offense to defense. To make matters worse, the coup in Egypt led Erdogan to reinterpret the domestic protests that had just occurred in Istanbul in late May, just a month before Morsi's overthrow. Erdogan linked the two processes in his mind, and became increasingly paranoid of domestic and foreign enemies that he suspected were working to undermine him.

Turkish Troubles and Erdogan's Paranoia

The downfall of Morsi in Egypt stands as the decisive moment in the civil war that gripped the Sunni world from 2012 to about 2020. Erdogan's Turkey emerged as the staunchest protagonist of the Brotherhood axis, now pitted openly against the conservative alliance led by the UAE and Saudi Arabia, supported by smaller powers like Jordan, Kuwait and Bahrain. With visions of grandeur, Erdogan had envisioned Turkey as the leader of new, more

Islamic Middle East run by populist, Islamist governments like his own. But this grandeur always masked a sense of vulnerability, one that would become apparent from 2013 to 2016 as Turkey limped from crisis to crisis. Moreover, while these crises were internal and largely the government's own doing, Erdogan would perceive them as tightly linked to the geopolitical struggle in the region, and as orchestrated by his foreign adversaries.

Erdogan has always been a highly polarizing figure in Turkey, regularly managing to obtain the support of a little over half of the population, while he is increasingly hated by the other half. He had battled the military and judiciary for decades to achieve and consolidate power, and knew that forces within the state would jump at the opportunity to unseat him. Being steeped deeply in the conspiratorial anti-Semitic environment of Turkish Islamism, Erdogan and many of his associates genuinely believed in the existence of a vast anti-Semitic conspiracy that would stop at nothing to undermine his noble vision.

In late May 2013, protests emerged in Istanbul over the planned urban development of a green area known as Gezi Park. These protests rapidly developed into a converging point for growing frustration with Erdogan's authoritarianism and Islamism among broad sections of urban Turkish society. But while some government representatives sought to assuage the protesters, Erdogan dismissed them as a bunch of looters, and sent in the riot police to deal with the problem. This led the protests to grow and to spread across the country. Seeing this rapid spread, Erdogan blamed the "interest rate lobby" for masterminding the protests. Lest anyone misinterpret the term, his deputy Prime

Minister explained that the "Jewish Diaspora," supposedly jealous of Turkey's economic growth, had been behind everything.[73]

Little wonder, then, that Erdogan similarly blamed the Jewish world conspiracy for the coup in Egypt.[74] To him, the events in Istanbul and Cairo appeared part of the same plot to undermine what his foreign minister Davutoğlu had termed an "axis" between Turkey and Cairo, which would be central to the future of the Middle East. Later, Davutoğlu explicitly linked the attempts to discredit Erdogan with the coup in Egypt – claiming that Morsi was unseated because the Gezi protests failed to unseat Erdogan.[75] Not too far in the future, they would view the 2016 coup attempt against Erdogan and the Gulf states' boycott of Qatar as part and parcel of the same conspiracy.

Erdoğan doubled down on his support for the Brotherhood, frequently appearing in public displaying the *rabaa* hand sign of the Muslim Brotherhood – flashing four fingers of the right hand with a folded-in thumb. Turkish leaders continued to take the lead in expressing outrage at the rise of Abdel Fattah al-Sisi to power in Egypt and the violent repression of the Muslim Brotherhood. Turkey welcomed thousands of Brotherhood exiles, and when Qatar relented to Gulf states' pressure to expel some Brotherhood figures, most moved to Turkey, where they established a large community and founded NGOs, websites, and television stations.[76]

Meanwhile, Erdogan was consumed by domestic matters.

---

73 Stuart Winer, "Turkish deputy PM blames Jews for Gezi protests," Times of Israel, July 2, 2013.

74 Gavriel Fiske, "Erdogan Accuses Israel of Engineering Egyptian Coup," August 20, 2013.

75 "Türkiye'de olmayınca Mısır'da darbe yaptılar," Sabah, May 17, 2015.

76 Ian Black, "Qatar-Gulf deal forces expulsion of Muslim Brotherhood leaders," Guardian, September 16, 2014. qatar-orders-expulsion-exiled-egyptian-muslim-brotherhood-leaders

As noted before, his rise to power had been facilitated by his tactical alliance with another fraternity – the religious community led by Pennsylvania-based preacher Fethullah Gülen. But once their alliance had succeeded in neutralizing the old Kemalist establishment through sham trials built by Gülenist prosecutors, they began to vie for power against each other. Erdogan was apprehensive that the Gülenists continued to maintain their separate networks and organizations, while Gülenists grew restless that Erdogan would not let them into the centers of political power. In 2012, Gülenist prosecutors took advantage of Erdogan undergoing a surgery to seek to interrogate his head of national intelligence, Hakan Fidan – a step that Erdogan saw as the start of a campaign against himself, and led to the beginning of bureaucratic trench warfare within the Turkish state.[77] In November 2013, prosecutors moved against several family members of close Erdogan confidants and cabinet members. The timing coincided with the release of secretly obtained documents and recordings that showed the involvement of these confidants in serious corruption. Four ministers resigned, and more were likely to be targeted – possibly including Erdogan's own family members – if Erdogan had not hit back by dismissing senior prosecutors and police officers involved in the investigations. As the struggle between Gülen and Erdogan deepened, Erdogan supporters seized on the fact that Gülen lived a reclusive life in the Poconos mountains in Pennsylvania to argue that the Gülen movement was connected to American intelligence structures – a belief that became widespread in Turkish society.

---

77   Halil Karaveli, "The Coalition Crumbles: Erdogan, the Gülenists, and Turkish Democracy," *Turkey Analyst,* February 20, 2012. (https://www.turkeyanalyst.org/publications/turkey-analyst-articles/item/395-the-coalition-crumbles-erdogan-the-g%C3%BClenists-and-turkish-democracy.html)

Neither side at the time understood that this Islamist civil war would bring to an end the ascendancy of Islamism as the dominant force in Turkish politics. In effect, it symbolized the collapse of the Turkish Islamist movement as a cohesive force. Against this background, a strange realignment took place in Turkish politics. Erdogan now turned to the secularist nationalists that he had only recently pushed either to the margins or thrown in jail, a marriage of convenience that only worked because these nationalists hated the Gülen movement more than they hated Erdogan. Hundreds of nationalist bureaucrats, military officers and intellectuals were released from prison, and rapidly obtained positions of influence filling offices vacated by the purge of Gülen sympathizers within the state institutions. In the political realm, Turkey's far-right nationalists – who had been in opposition to Erdogan – now joined forces with him, and endorsed the transformation of the political system from a parliamentary to a presidential one. This planted the seeds for the nationalist realignment that began soon thereafter, discussed in a later chapter.

Meanwhile, in October 2014, Erdogan introduced the term "üst akıl," translated as "mastermind," as the nebulous force that was trying to keep Turkey down. Again, in case anyone had misunderstood, a pro-government television channel produced a two-hour documentary on how the Jews had sought world domination for the past 3,500 years.[78]

Then, on July 15, 2016, elements in the Turkish army outside of the chain of command staged a coup attempt against President Erdogan. This coup attempt took place just ahead of a scheduled

78   "Islamist Turkish President Erdogan Says a 'Mastermind' Is Plotting Against
        Turkey; Antisemitic 'Documentary' Says Jews Have Been 'Mastermind' For
        Over 3,500 Years," MEMRI, April 14, 2015. (https://www.memri.org/reports/
        islamist-turkish-president-erdogan-says-mastermind-plotting-against-turkey-antisemitic)

major purge of Gülenists from army ranks. Many of the details of this coup attempt remain murky – for example, it is clear that there was a genuine if botched coup attempt. It is not entirely clear, however, whether the government purposefully provoked the coup attempt – signaling an imminent purge in order to smoke out Gülen sympathizers from the military. What is clear is that the only organized force in the military that had the capacity to organize a coup attempt outside of the chain of command was the Gülen fraternity. In the process, many non-aligned officers appear to have rolled the dice and sided either with Erdogan or with the coup plotters, in the latter case sealing their fate when the coup failed.

Americans and Europeans tend to underestimate the impact of this coup attempt on both Erdogan and Turkish society at large. The strength of the Gülenists within the military surprised everyone, and the Obama Administration's slow and equivocal response to the coup heightened suspicions that America somehow had a hand in it. To Turkish leaders that were already primed to think in terms of large conspiracies, it seemed unthinkable that such a powerful force could have emerged inside the Turkish state without foreign direction.

This domestic Turkish turmoil took place in parallel with the fallout of the Syrian civil war, which boosted the Kurdish nationalist movement in Turkey. The Islamic State's siege of Kobane in northern Syria, and Turkey's indifference to the jihadist movement, which it viewed as a lesser threat than the Syrian Kurds, led to massive mobilization among Turkish Kurds in favor of the pro-Kurdish HDP party in the June 2015 elections. It also put America's collusion with the Kurds in a new light for Turkish nationalists. The dividing lines between the domestic and the foreign had largely disappeared.

The Qatar Crisis: The Sunni Rift Deepens

The rift within the Sunni world would deepen in 2017, for a variety of reasons. For one, by mid-2017, Turkey had overcome its internal turmoil. Following the July 2016 coup attempt, Erdogan purged thousands of Gülen sympathizers from government service, and engineered a referendum to transform Turkey's political system into a presidential one – thus consolidating power in his own hands and emerging stronger and more assertive on the international scene. More importantly perhaps, Donald Trump took office in the United States in January 2017, and made a U-turn in U.S. policy toward Iran.

Under Obama, as will be discussed in detail in the next chapter, the U.S. had single-mindedly pursued the objective of normalizing U.S. relations with Iran. Obama officials have acknowledged that Iran was the single most important issue in Obama's second term, equating it in importance to the emphasis on healthcare in domestic affairs.[79] While the proximate goal was an agreement on the Iranian nuclear weapons program, the broader ambition was to transform the situation in the Middle East by bringing Iran back in from the cold – transforming Iran from a spoiler seeking to undermine regional stability into a more cooperative force. Michael Doran summarizes the philosophy of Obama as follows:

---

79   Matthew Continetti, "The Coming Détente with Iran," *Washington Free Beacon*, October 31, 2014. (https://freebeacon.com/columns/the-coming-detente-with-iran/)

If, in Bushland, America had behaved like a sheriff, assembling a posse ("a coalition of the willing") to go in search of monsters, in Obamaworld America would disarm its rivals by ensnaring them in a web of cooperation. To rid the world of rogues and tyrants, one must embrace and soften them.[80]

This approach put the Sunni powers on guard, as the results of the U.S.-Iranian dance would affect their security in fundamental ways. But with Trump in power, the U.S. administration made it clear it would not honor Obama's nuclear deal with Iran, and would instead return to contain Iran and seek to roll back its regional influence. President Trump made Saudi Arabia the destination of his first foreign trip in May 2017, a trip during which he signed a $100 billion arms deal with the Kingdom, and took part in a summit of Arab and Muslim leaders. He also took part in the inauguration of a new center to combat Islamic extremism.

Two weeks after Trump's visit, Saudi Arabia, the UAE, Bahrein and Egypt cut diplomatic ties with Qatar, closed their airspace to Qatar-bound flights, and imposed a blockade on the small emirate. They issued a thirteen-part list of demands on Qatar to normalize relations. These demands focused on ending Qatar's support for the Muslim Brotherhood and other extremist groups, curtailing its relations with Iran, and ending the Turkish military presence in Qatar.

This Turkish base had been opened in April 2016, in order to oppose "common enemies" of the two states and contribute to

80   Michael Doran, "Obama's Secret Iran Strategy," *Mosaic*, February 2, 2015. (https://www. hudson.org/foreign-policy/obama-s-secret-iran-strategy)

stability in the Gulf.[81] In part, it was seen as a move to shore up Qatar against Iran, given the joint Turkish and Qatari support for Syrian opposition forces fighting against Iranian ally Bashar al-Assad – at a time when the Obama Administration appeared an unreliable protector of Gulf states against Iranian encroachment. But given the deepening rift among the Sunni powers, the Turkish move appeared also directed against the UAE and Saudi Arabia.

Erdogan had further reasons to back Qatar. The day after the failed July 2016 coup, Sheikh Tamim had dispatched special forces to protect President Erdogan – who feared that his own security detail may have been infiltrated by coup-plotters.[82] This strengthened the bond between the two members of the Brotherhood axis – while the coup worsened Turkish relations with the UAE, which Ankara blamed for having supported the coup.

Therefore, when Qatar was in need, Turkey responded immediately. Two days following the ultimatum, the Turkish parliament ratified two separate treaties on military cooperation with Qatar, and sent military materiel to the Turkish base in Qatar – which would gradually grow to host 5,000 troops, almost half the number of the large American Al Udeid air base not far away. Turkey also resolutely helped Qatar overcome the boycott by shipping in food and commodities by air and sea. Turkey played an absolute crucial role in helping the Qatari Emir survive the onslaught from his neighbors, and – some analysts think – helped forestall a Saudi-led attempt to overthrow the Emir.

---

81   Heather Murdock, "Turkey Opens First Mideast Military Base in Qatar" VOA, May 10, 2016. (https://www.voanews.com/a/turkey-opens-first-middle-east-military-base-in-qatar/3323653.html)

82   "Qatar sent forces to protect Erdogan after coup attempt," *Middle East Monitor*, February 2, 2017. (https://www.middleeastmonitor.com/20170202-qatar-sent-forces-to-protect-erdogan-after-coup-attempt/)
      https://www.middleeastmonitor.com/20170202-qatar-sent-forces-to-protect-erdogan-after-coup-attempt/

Unsurprisingly, Iran stepped in to assist Qatar as well. While Doha and Tehran have their differences, Iran could not pass up an opportunity to counter the efforts of Saudi Arabia and the UAE to expand their regional influence. Iranian exports to Qatar quadrupled, and Iran's airspace allowed for Qatar airways to continue to operate. It soon became clear that the blockade of Qatar had failed and, if anything, strengthened Iran's regional influence while solidifying the Brotherhood axis. Inadvertently, the conservative Sunni powers helped bridge the differences created in Syria between the Brotherhood axis and Iran.

Turkey's role in coming to Qatar's rescue led to a sharp deterioration of ties with the UAE and Saudi Arabia. Ankara was particularly rattled by the elevation of Mohammed bin Salman as Crown Prince, which took place in late June 2017, two weeks after the beginning of the Qatar crisis. The reason was the Crown Prince's new policies on religious and social matters.

In October 2017, Mohammed bin Salman announced his intention to reverse Saudi Arabia's course in religious affairs. As has been seen, he condemned Saudi support for extremist Wahhabi ideology during the past thirty years as something "not normal," as an unfortunate reaction to the Iranian revolution. He promised to return Saudi Arabia to "moderate Islam" and to destroy extremist thought "now and immediately."[83] Not long after, Saudi Arabia's Grand Mufti declared Hamas a terrorist

---

83   Martin Chulov, "I Will Return Saudi Arabia to Moderate Islam, Says Crown Prince," *Guardian*, October 24, 2017. (https://www.theguardian.com/world/2017/oct/24/i-will-return-saudi-arabia-moderate-islam-crown-prince)

organization and issued a fatwa "forbidding the fight against the Jews and forbidding to kill them."[84]

This was a major shift, and it did not go down well in Ankara, where it was seen as an extension of the global anti-Islamic conspiracy. Erdoğan severely castigated Saudi Arabia's reforms and rejected Mohammed bin Sultan's notion of "moderate Islam." Erdoğan called this is a foreign invention and a "trap to weaken Islam," and AKP mouthpieces went farther. The Islamist daily *Yeni Şafak's* lead editor Ibrahim Karagül called Saudi reforms a "very dangerous game," that he claimed was instigated by the United States and Israel, an "American plan whose final aim is to occupy Islam's holy sites, Mecca and Medina."[85]

The next year, relations turned even worse following the murder of Saudi Muslim Brotherhood activist and journalist Jamal Khashoggi at the Saudi consulate in Istanbul. Turkish authorities were understandably incensed by the event, but decided to use Khashoggi's tragic fate to its advantage by gradually, slowly, but surely releasing incriminating evidence to the world media – and adding lurid details to further paint Saudi Arabia and Mohammed bin Salman personally in the worst possible light.

The Anti-Turkish Coalition Emerges

While Turkey's relations with the conservative Sunni powers worsened, it found itself increasingly isolated in the Eastern

84   "Israel Welcomes Saudi Mufti's pro-Israel Remarks, Invites Him to Visit the Country," *Anadolu Ajansi*, November 14, 2017. (https://www.dailysabah.com/mideast/2017/11/14/israel-welcomes-saudi-muftis-pro-israel-remarks-invites-him-to-visit-the-country)

85   Svante E. Cornell, "Turkish-Saudi Rivalry: Behind the Khashoggi Affair," *The American Interest*, November 9, 2018. (https://www.the-american-interest.com/2018/11/06/behind-the-khashoggi-affair/)

Mediterranean as well. In the early 2010s, vast reserves of natural gas were discovered in the Eastern Mediterranean, roughly speaking in the waters between Egypt and Cyprus. While the gas resources closer to Egypt were not disputed in any way, those nearer to Cyprus were, because of the unresolved nature of the Cyprus conflict. Following Turkey's invasion of Cyprus in 1974, a Turkish Republic of Northern Cyprus was proclaimed, which is recognized only by Turkey. Yet the rest of the world views the Greek Cypriot government as the legitimate government of Cyprus – and thus of the gas resources. Ankara, however, objected that any energy development would have to await a formal resolution to the Cyprus dispute.

Turkey also long pursued an eccentric interpretation of legal rights to undersea resources. Its position stems from the multitude of Greek islands in almost direct juxtaposition to the long Turkish coastline. As a result, applying the principles of the Law of the Sea convention to the Aegean (that is, territorial waters of 12 nautical miles and exclusive economic zones of up to 200 nm) would essentially give Greece total control over the Aegean, and confine Turkey to being an inland power. In opposition to this, Turkey announced in the mid-1990s that the extension of Greek territorial waters from 6 to 12 nautical miles would constitute a *casus belli* – a cause for war – and Ankara further argued that principles of equity require that islands not be given the same rights as regular coastlines. Thus, according to the Turkish view, Greek islands would be entitled only to a narrow territorial waters of six nautical miles, and the continental shelf surrounding them should be considered Turkish. The Law of the Sea convention default position, by contrast, gives the same rights to islands as to landmasses, and would therefore give Greece much greater control over both the sea and is subsea resources.

The EU's decision to include Cyprus as a member state in 2004– in spite of the Greek Cypriot administration's opposition to a UN plan to resolve the conflict – effectively made the EU a party to the dispute. Greek Cypriot authorities were now able to represent Cyprus in the EU, liberally using their newly won veto powers to influence EU policy. This was met with alarm in Turkey; particularly in the Turkish navy, which saw a great danger in the EU adopting Greek views on the maritime delimitation in the Aegean. From this emerged a doctrine known as "Mavi Vatan" or "Blue Homeland," which assertively pushed the Turkish definition of its rights over the continental shelf, ignoring the Greek islands. Admiral Cem Gürdeniz, the originator of the doctrine, defines the Blue Homeland as "an extension at sea and seabed of our homeland located between 26-45 East longitudes and 36-42 North latitudes. The Blue Homeland is the name of our zone of interest and jurisdiction located between 25-45 East longitudes and 33-43 North latitudes."[86] This remained an assertive but fringe view among Turkish nationalist circles. But in the nationalist frenzy following the 2016 failed coup, its proponents suddenly gained influence and were able to make the Blue Homeland doctrine state policy.

Thus from 2018 onward, the controversies over the Eastern Mediterranean merged with Turkey's troubles with Middle Eastern powers. One important area where this played out was Libya, where Turkey had an agenda that diverged substantially from that of Egypt, Saudi Arabia and the UAE. Turkey was drawn to the

---

86   Cem Gürdeniz, "What is the Blue Homeland in the 21st century?" UWI Data, July 31, 2020.
      (https://uwidata.com/12952-what-is-the-blue-homeland-in-the-21st-century/)

Muslim Brotherhood-dominated General National Congress, and from 2015 the interim government known as the Government of National Accord, (GNA) which gained UN recognition, in which Brotherhood forces continued to exert influence. Meanwhile, Egypt, Saudi Arabia and the UAE endorsed the alternative government loyal to the Tobruk-based Libyan House of Representatives, which in turn had appointed Field Marshal Khalifa Haftar as head of the Libyan National Army (LNA). Haftar, a Qaddafi-era military officer who turned against Qaddafi in the late 1980s, had repressed the various extremist Islamist groups that had emerged in eastern Libya, ingratiating himself with Egypt and the UAE. As the Libyan civil war intensified, the UAE and Egypt provided weapons, arms, and mercenaries to the LNA as it sought to make a push to take over the Libyan capital, Tripoli.

Turkey was alarmed by this development, seeing it as an extension of the "counter-revolution" sponsored by the conservative Sunni powers. And thus, the Libyan civil war essentially became a proxy war in the conflict tearing apart the Sunni world. For Turkey, however, Libya held an additional value because of its Mediterranean coastline. With a little bit of creativity, one could design a map of the continental shelves along the Mediterranean and find a spot where the claims of Turkey and Libya meet. Of course, to do this one would have to essentially claim the waters off Greek islands like Rhodes and Crete as Turkish, and Libya would have to adopt the Turkish view of maritime law and ignore the large island of Crete, thus laying claim to large parts of Greece's exclusive economic zone. This is exactly what Admiral Gürdeniz had done – but understandably, the Libyan government had been reluctant to do this, as it would be sure to undermine its relations with the EU and its broader international standing. But beggars cannot be choosers, and when the GNA government found itself under attack from Haftar and his Gulf supporters, it finally relented and signed a maritime agreement with Turkey in November 2019, effectively endorsing Turkey's interpretation of maritime law. Ankara reciprocated by a major military intervention that succeeded in pushing back Haftar's forces, thwarting the Saudi-Emirati-Egyptian effort to assert control over Libya. This was a major success for Turkey, which for the first time showed its expeditionary capabilities, including roundly defeating Russian Wagner contractors that the UAE had bankrolled to fight alongside Haftar's forces.[87]

However, Turkey's wins in Libya were not mirrored in the Eastern Mediterranean. Ankara responded to Greek and Cypriot energy initiatives by dispatching gunboats to prevent the further exploration by energy companies in disputed areas. Meanwhile, Ankara acquired two large drilling vessels and began unilaterally engaging in its own gas exploration projects in areas claimed by the Greek Cypriot government. Now, Turkey's Middle Eastern and European foes found common cause – as the UAE and Saudi Arabia rapidly developed military and security ties with Greece and Cyprus. Saudi and Emirati air force units became frequent participants in military exercises in Greece, and in August 2020, the UAE dispatched several F-16 fighter jets to the Greek island of Crete as a show of support during an uptick in ten-

---

87   Ben Fishman, "Libya's Armed Group Catch-22," Washington Institute for Near East
      Policy, February 15, 2024. (https://www.washingtoninstitute.org/policy-analysis/
      libyas-armed-group-catch-22)

sions between Greece and Turkey. That October, Greece and the UAE signed a Strategic Partnership Agreement that contained a mutual defense clause.[88]

Meanwhile, the states opposing Turkish ambitions organized themselves in the East Mediterranean Gas Forum, formally created in 2020. This structure brought together Israel, the Palestinian Authority, Cyprus, Egypt and Greece, alongside Italy and France. Notably the organization did not extend an invitation to Ankara to join, instead developing into a coordination mechanism on energy issues that would deny Turkey the regional powerhouse role it sought. In particular, the involvement of several EU states in the Forum created new headaches for Turkey, as France in particular involved itself deeply in the matter, not least on account of the leading role of French energy companies in exploration projects led by Greek Cyprus. France's navy became a regular presence in Cypriot waters, further increasing the risk of escalation in the standoff between Turkey and nearly a dozen powers with diverse background and goals. While these states had little in common, they united in opposing Turkish ambitions, leading to a very detrimental situation for Ankara. Its adversaries deepened their cooperation in all areas and worked jointly to lobby against Turkish interests in Washington D.C. as well as in Brussels.

---

88   Paul Iddon, "How Significant Is Greece's Growing Military Cooperation With The UAE And Saudi Arabia?," *Forbes*, March 31, 2021. (https://www.forbes.com/sites/pauliddon/2021/03/31/how-significant-is-greeces-growing-military-cooperation-with-the-uae-and-saudi-arabia/?sh=1401409e19ef); Ed Adamczyk, "Greece, UAE agree to mutual defense pact," UPI, November 23, 2020. (https://www.upi.com/Defense-News/2020/11/23/Greece-UAE-agree-to-mutual-defense-pact/6791606163106/)

The End of the Road

The period from 2013-20, roughly speaking, was characterized by a deepening split within the Sunni Muslim world, pitting the Brotherhood axis against a conservative alliance. This conflict began with the overthrow of Mohammed Morsi, and grew more intense, spreading out to the Eastern Mediterranean and involving European powers – while confronting the United States with a headache. But this period would give way to a more cooperative environment in the years that followed, as a result of several factors. These included the return of Joe Biden to the White House along with much of the foreign policy thinking that had dominated in the Obama administration; but other factors included the continued Iranian belligerence, as well as domestic changes in Turkey, which found itself increasingly isolated and embarked upon a significant shift away from its earlier priorities. In many ways, the Brotherhood axis would admit defeat and Turkey would drop the most ideological aspects of its foreign policy.

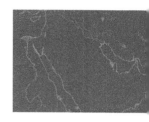

11.
AMERICA'S DANCE WITH IRAN

America's relationship with Iran has been a huge source of instability in Middle East geopolitics. If Iran is the prime mover of Middle Eastern geopolitics, as we have seen, the U.S. served as the key counter-balancing force against Iranian ambitions since the founding of the Islamic republic in 1979. More recently, regional states, beginning with Israel, have increasingly come to question the reliability of the U.S. resolve to oppose Iran. As the Iranian nuclear weapons program progressed in the early 2000s, the U.S. repeatedly issued a commitment to ensure that Iran does not acquire nuclear weapons. Yet in 2022, the Institute for Science and International Security announced that it now assessed Iran's breakout timeline – the time until Iran has sufficient nuclear material to build a bomb – to zero. To make matters worse, the U.S. has alternated between hard pressure – as in Trump's "maximum pressure" campaign – and policies that sought to appease Tehran and work to integrate it into the international system. These 180-degree turns have done little to reassure American allies and partners in the region. Furthermore, they have sent the signal to Iran that American pressure may last only until the next U.S. election, and that the same may be true for diplomatic initiatives.

Obama's Vision

Barack Obama came into Washington with a derisive view of the foreign policy establishment in the capital, which his closest associates referred to as the "blob." Whereas earlier administrations had interacted closely with the Washington think tank community, the Obama foreign policy team did not – it relied on a small number of handpicked experts close to its own way of viewing the world. Key to this worldview was that many of America's problems in the world were a result of America's own policies and actions, not of those of America's adversaries. This was a particularly strong sentiment at the time of Obama's election, a time dominated by the fallout of the Bush Administration's decision to invade Iraq and topple Saddam Hussein.

Colored perhaps by the Iraq debacle, Obama and his closest entourage appeared to be motivated by a conviction that U.S. intervention abroad almost automatically leads to embroilment in long and devastating military operations. Further, they appeared convinced that U.S. interventions abroad tended to make things worse rather than better.[89] As Edward Lucas summarized the Obama Administration's thinking with regard to Eastern Europe, there was a prevalent belief that American engagement

---

89   See discussion in Stephen Blank, "Missing in Action: U.S. Policy," in Svante E. Cornell, eds., *The International Politics of the Armenia–Azerbaijan Conflict*, New York: Palgrave, 2017, pp. 125-148.

"is increasingly irrelevant. Or counter-productive. Or expensive. Or useless."[90]

The Obama notion was, furthermore, that regions like eastern Europe and the Middle East were troublesome areas with little upside for the United States. Europe was "done," and could be left to the Europeans. Obama scoffed at Mitt Romney's accurate assertion in the 2012 electoral campaign that Russia was America's "number one geopolitical foe," laughingly quipping that the 1980s were calling and wanted their foreign policy back.[91] Similarly, Obama viewed the Middle East as increasingly irrelevant in an era where fossil fuels were bound to lose their importance, and where America was being dragged into controversy by needy dependents like Israel and the Gulf States. Instead, America would "Pivot to Asia," where the challenges and opportunities of the future lay. Not staying at that, America under his leadership made clear his administration would work on big, global matters like climate change and Obama's personal favorite – nuclear disarmament.

This forms the background for the Obama Administration's policy in the region. Washington needed to change the geopolitics in the Middle East by creating an order that would allow it to leave the region to be handled by regional powers. As Obama once put it, the Saudis would have to "share the neighborhood" with Iran. That required transforming the current situation where America was being pulled in by the likes of Israel and Saudi Arabia into an anti-Iranian coalition. Instead, America would

90   Edward Lucas, "Getting It Right on Ukraine: Realpolitik vs. Wishful Thinking," *Center for European Policy Analysis*, January 28, 2014. (https://cepa.ecms.pl/index/?id=d5e9d9e23447e1907c70ac5d9b29edcc)

91   Jillian Rayfield, "Obama: The '80s Called, They Want their Foreign Policy Back," *Salon*, October 23, 2012.

seek to find ways to bring Iran into a more constructive role that would avert the need for an anti-Iran coalition in the first place. The key to doing this was to push for an agreement on the Iranian nuclear program, parking that issue so that a normalization with Iran could take place.

Obama's idea was not new. Advocates for diplomatic engagement with Iran had been making their case in Washington for a long time. They got a shot in the arm when the Iraq Study Group, led by former Indiana Congressman Lee Hamilton and former Secretary of State James Baker, issued a report in 2006 that made the case for America to launch a diplomatic engagement of the Islamic Republic.[92] This report was published the same year that Obama arrived in Washington as a Senator, and appears to have influenced his thinking. He drew close collaborators from the Study Group, including Ben Rhodes, the writer of much of the report.

It should be recalled that this was the time just before the Bush Administration's surge in Iraq, which stabilized the ill-fated invasion somewhat. Criticism of the Bush Administration's foreign policy was widespread because of the Iraq debacle; moreover, views of Iran were affected by the recency of the September 11 attacks, and the continued threat of Sunni jihadism. America's relationship with Saudi Arabia was strained by the fact that the large majority of the 9/11 hijackers were Saudi, and many were pointing fingers at the Kingdom's role in midwifing Salafi-Jihadi movements across the globe. Against this background, there was a growing sentiment that America's main problem might be Sunni extremism, and that Washington and Tehran thus shared the

---

92   James A. Baker, III, and Lee H. Hamilton, *The Iraq Study Group Report*, New York: Vintage Books, 2006, pp. 50-54.

same enemy. Obviously, there may also have been a healthy dose of nostalgia for the pre-1979 situation when Iran was America's main partner in the Middle East. Ignoring the reality of Tehran's ambitions – and the centrality of opposition to America in the regime's ideology – many were lured to think that an outreach to Iran could yield benefits for America.

The Iran Deal and Obama's Deference to Tehran

The agreement the Obama Administration had in mind was one that focused solely on the nuclear issue. It therefore explicitly left out Iran's active backing of international terrorism and its support for armed proxies across the region that destabilized neighboring states. It would not even touch Iran's role in killing American soldiers in Iraq. This approach would not have been possible if the core problem was identified to be Iran's hegemonic ambitions across the Middle East. But it made sense if the problem was seen to be America's pressure on Iran, which some saw as contributing to a siege mentality among Tehran's leaders – which in turn triggered Tehran to lash out the way it did. Indeed, the Iraq Study Group report repeatedly stressed Iran's fear that America sought regime change in Iran as an impediment to diplomatic initiatives.

This approach on the part of the Obama Administration was not limited to Iran: similar thinking animated its approach to Russia. Only months after Russia's invasion of Georgia, Obama pushed for a "Reset" of relations with Moscow that aimed to – unsurprisingly – reassure Russian leaders that America harbored no ill intentions toward them. In both situations, this required American restraint in order not to upset fickle rulers in Moscow or Tehran. In the Russian case, it meant avoiding American entanglements in what Russia considered its "near abroad," as such moves could "irritate Russia." In the Middle East, it similarly meant to avoid making moves that would step on perceived Iranian red lines – such as Syria or Hezbollah. But unlike in the Russia case, the Obama Administration utilized a host of instruments of economic pressure to bring Iran to the negotiating table. In 2010, while holding the door open for diplomacy, Obama approved sanctions on Iran's oil and gas sector that he termed the "toughest ever."[93] This built some credibility for the Administration to approach the Iranian regime and force it to an agreement that would put a temporary halt to its nuclear program.

Still, the Obama Administration knew its policy would be roundly condemned as appeasement of Iran by the Republican opposition, and key parts of the Democratic leadership in Congress. In fact, some of the specifics of the nuclear agreement were mind-boggling.[94] The most obvious examples are the multiple "sunset provisions" in the deal, that is, most restrictions on Iran's nuclear program would gradually evaporate with time. This suggested the deal was simply intended to kick the can down the road and hand the problem of Iran's nuclear weapons over to some later administration. Already after ten years, the UN Security Council would "end consideration" of Iran's nuclear program, and the possibility of imposing "snapback sanctions" if Iran violated the agreement would disappear. After fifteen years, almost all restrictions on Iranian research on, as well as enrichment and

---

93   Ross Colvin, "Obama Says New U.S. Sanctions on Iran Toughest Ever," Reuters, July 2, 2010. (https://www.reuters.com/article/idUSTRE66001Z/)

94   Mark Dubowitz and Annie Fixler, *The Iran Deal's Fatal Flaws After One Year: Emboldened Iran and Diminished American Deterrence*, FDD Press, July 2016. (https://www.fdd.org/wp-content/uploads/2016/07/Dubowitz-Fixler-Fatal-Flaws-After-One-Year.pdf)

stockpiling of nuclear materials would end. And the benefits to Iran of essentially promising to, perhaps, delay its nuclear program somewhat, were plentiful. Iran obtained billions and billions of dollars in frozen Iranian assets, funds that went directly to its regional hegemonic agenda, not to economic and social needs of Iranian citizens.

Not staying at that, the deal obligated the U.S. and Western partners to help Iran develop in the areas of energy, finance, technology and trade. As Robert Satloff has observed, "the idea that America and its allies will actually help Iran grow stronger in these areas will sound a discordant note around the Middle East," given that it forces America to assist Iran in spite of its nefarious actions against America's allies and partners.[95]

No wonder the Administration had to engage in various types of subterfuge in order to "sell" the agreement to a doubtful public. To begin with, it claimed that the opportunity for a nuclear deal came as the result of the election of "moderate" candidate Hassan Rouhani in 2013, and that a deal would embolden reformers in Iran. In reality, the Administration had held secret talks with Iran already in 2012, in which the main elements of the nuclear deal were hammered out. The reference to Rouhani's election was deliberately crafted to make the agreement less controversial at home.[96] It also ignored the fact that Iranian foreign policy is made by the Supreme Leader, not the country's President, and that the Supreme Leader has ultimate authority over approving presidential candidates. Similarly, the Administration,

---

95   Robert Satloff, "What's Really Wrong with the Iran Nuclear Deal," Washington Institute, July 14, 2015. (https://www.washingtoninstitute.org/policy-analysis/whats-really-wrong-iran-nuclear-deal)

96   David Samuels, "The Aspiring Novelist Who Became Obama's Foreign-Policy Guru," *The New York Times Magazine*, May 5, 2016.

and particularly Deputy National Security Advisor Ben Rhodes, went to great lengths in misrepresenting the nature of the deal once it was finalized in 2015. Their efforts to do so went so far that the Iranians publicly slammed the Administration's readout of the agreement's provisions. Most importantly, the Administration hammered home a binary choice – a false one, many would argue – that the only alternative to the agreement was to go to war with Iran. With a war-weary population at home, this argument proved effective as detractors to the deal never mustered a serious response that explained how they would achieve a better result without resorting to force.

Iran, after signing the deal, made it clear it would view the imposition of *any* sanctions as a violation, triggering the snapback of its nuclear program. Meanwhile, in 2016 German authorities warned that the Iranian regime actively went about searching for materials for the nuclear program that was supposed to be on hold.[97] The Obama Administration also went to great lengths to avoid confrontation with Iran both during the negotiation of the agreement and after the signing of the deal. A 2016 report from the Institute for Science and International Security concluded that "the Obama administration has inhibited federal investigations and prosecutions of alleged Iranian illegal procurement efforts. The stated reason has been concern about the impact on the Iran nuclear deal."[98] In other words, the perceived need to protect the agreement with Iran – and the President's signature

---

97   Polina Garaev, "Iran still trying to acquire materials for nuclear program, Germany warns," I24News, July 7, 2016. (https://www.i24news.tv/en/news/international/119127-160707-iran-still-trying-to-acquire-materials-for-nuclear-program-germany-warns)

98   David Albright and Andrea Stricker, "Previously Sanctioned Iranian Entities Doing Business in China," Institute for Science and International Security, July 7, 2016. (https://isis-online.org/uploads/isis-reports/documents/Previously_Sanctioned_Iranian_Entities_Doing_Business_in_China_7Jul2016_Final.pdf)

accomplishment – went so far that the Administration sought to put the brakes on efforts to go after Iranian attempts to circumvent the agreement.

The story of Project Cassandra is perhaps even more damning. Led by the U.S. Drug Enforcement Agency, a task force comprising several agencies of the U.S. government worked for several years on a complex investigation of Lebanese Hezbollah. The Task Force revealed that Hezbollah had developed into a major force in international organized crime, and was deeply involved in the smuggling of cocaine and other narcotics, as well as in laundering billions of dollars of drug money. But as Josh Meyer at *Politico* details in an extensive exposé, the task force ran into trouble when its investigations led it to central actors in the core of the Hezbollah network, including the key middleman linking Hezbollah to Iran, the Obama Justice Department moved in to stop the DEA efforts to intervene.[99] As Katherine Bauer, a former Treasury official, testified to Congress in 2017, Hezbollah "investigations were tamped down for fear of rocking the boat with Iran and jeopardizing the nuclear deal."[100]

It is also obvious that such considerations were key to Obama's reluctance, in 2013, to enforce his own stated "red line" and intervene against the Syrian regime following its use of chemical weapons to target civilians in a rebel-held suburb of Damascus. While this was in part a result of Obama wanting to avoid an entanglement in Syria dominating his second term in

---

99   Josh Meyer, "The Secret Backstory of How Obama Let Hezbollah Off the Hook," *Politico*, December 2017. (https://www.politico.com/interactives/2017/obama-hezbollah-drug-trafficking-investigation/)

100   Katherine Bauer, "Iran on Notice," Testimony to the House Committee on Foreign Affairs, February 16, 2017. (https://www.documentcloud.org/documents/4329058-Katherine-Bauer-testimony-to-the-House-Committee.html)

office, it was also a function of Iranian and U.S. officials having informed him in no uncertain terms that doing so would kill the prospects of a nuclear deal with Tehran.[101]

No wonder, thus, that analysts like Michael Doran have concluded that the Iran deal was the result not of mishaps or the lack of strategy, but very much the result of a clear but unspoken strategic realignment of American's relations with the broader Middle East.[102] In this strategy, America would actively work for the reintegration of Iran in the region as a constructive regional power. Unfortunately, Iran did not reciprocate and lower tensions with its neighbors or the West – it pushed forward with its efforts to seek regional hegemony. This left the nuclear agreement highly vulnerable – because Obama had deliberately designed it in such a way that it would not require congressional approval. This meant it was entirely dependent on the U.S. executive continuing to support the agreement – it was not a treaty that the U.S. was legally bound to follow.[103]

Trump's Maximum Pressure

Obama's Iran deal was faced with a storm of criticism, not least as any expectation that it would lead to a moderation of Iran's nefarious activities across the region were proven wrong. Quite to the contrary, Iran redoubled its efforts to expand its influence from the Mediterranean across the Middle East to Yemen. In the

101 Jay Solomon, *The Iran Wars*, New York: Random House, 2016.

102 Michael Doran, "Obama's Secret Iran Strategy," *Mosaic*, February 2, 2015. (https://www.hudson.org/foreign-policy/obama-s-secret-iran-strategy)

103 Suzanne Maloney, "Trump Could Gut the Iran Deal—But it Was Vulnerable All Along," Brookings, November 17, 2016. (https://www.brookings.edu/articles/trump-could-gut-the-iran-deal-but-it-was-vulnerable-all-along/)

2016 election, Republican candidates uniformly condemned the Iran deal, terming it an American capitulation to Iran's regional ambitions. Opinions varied on whether the U.S. should summarily leave the agreement, or whether it should seek to renegotiate the agreement.

When Trump took office in January 2017, he surrounded himself with a national security team that, as Brookings expert Suzanne Maloney put it, shared "an Iran-centric interpretation of the problems that plague the Middle East and threaten vital American interests there."[104] More specifically, the Trump Administration differed from its predecessor by not being laser-focused on the nuclear issue, as Obama had been – something that led his administration to view the survival of the agreement as a primary objective. The Trump Administration instead saw the broader issue of Iran's attempts at regional hegemony as the main target of its policies.

Still, it took time before the Trump Administration was able to articulate concrete policies toward the Middle East – or anything, for that matter. The chaos and in-fighting of the Trump Administration is stuff of legends. The Trump campaign, it appears, did not expect to win the 2016 election and had not prepared for the transition to the presidency. National security staffing was a problem. Trump's first National Security Advisor Michael J. Flynn lasted for three weeks, while his successor, H.R. McMaster, stayed in the job for little over a year. Secretary of State Rex Tillerson served a year before being showed the door. The problem was even bigger at lower-level positions, as the Trump Administration

---

104 Suzanne Maloney, "Under Trump, U.S. Policy on Iran is Moving from Accommodation to Confrontation," Brookings, May 11, 2017. (https://www.brookings.edu/articles/under-trump-u-s-policy-on-iran-is-moving-from-accommodation-to-confrontation/)

failed to get officials confirmed, and in some cases, to even put forward nominations for important positions. National Security staff had to deal with the erratic nature of the President, and the involvement of his close family members – particularly his son-in-law Jared Kushner – in foreign policy. Kushner would ultimately play a positive role in helping negotiate the Abraham Accords, but the chaos of the Administration meant that it took a long time for serious Iran policy to develop.

Only in a May 2018 speech, following the announcement that the U.S. withdrew from the Iran nuclear deal, did Secretary of State Mike Pompeo announce a new Iran strategy. This strategy was focused on a containment and rolling back of Iran's regional ambition, including what Pompeo termed "unprecedented financial pressure on the Iranian regime." Summarizing the American objective, Pompeo quipped that the Iranian regime had been "fighting all over the Middle East for years. After our sanctions come in force, it will be battling to keep its economy alive."[105] In addition to putting pressure on the regime, the policy sought to deter Iranian aggression, as well as advocate for the Iranian people. In other words, it was a strategy that sought to force Iran to renege on its effort to build regional hegemony.

In some ways, the strategy worked. By 2020, the Iranian leadership conceded that the Trump policies had cost Iran $200 billion, and Iranian foreign currency reserves had plummeted from $122 billion in 2018 to just $4 billion.[106] Had Trump been re-elected and his policies been sustained, it is possible that his

---

105　"After the Deal: A New Iran Strategy," Heritage Foundation, May 21, 2018

106　Elliot Abrams, "Did the "Maximum Pressure" Campaign Against Iran Fail?" Council on Foreign Relations, July 12, 2021. (https://www.cfr.org/blog/did-maximum-pressure-campaign-against-iran-fail)

"maximum pressure" would have forced the Iranian regime to make concessions in order to survive, and that it would have been unable to fund its expensive imperialist project across the region. But because the Administration wasted a year and a half before adopting this strategy, it provided Iran with the hope that it might just be able to hold out long enough to see a Democratic Administration return to power in Washington.

Meanwhile, in the short term Iran raised the stakes. In 2019, it embarked on a series of moves that were designed to test American resolve, while maintaining "plausible deniability." This included attacking four commercial ships in the Emirati port of Fujairah in May 2019. The U.S. government, following a brief investigation, nevertheless attributed the attack to the IRGC.[107] In September 2019, a drone attack targeted a Saudi oil facility in Abqaiq, which temporarily suspended the flow of 5.7 million barrels of oil per day – half of the Kingdom's production. While the Yemeni Houthis happily claimed responsibility for the attack, U.S. intelligence concluded the attack came from the north. American officials leaked information to the media that America had intelligence showing satellite imagery of IRGC forces preparing the attack from a military base in Ahvaz, in southern Iran.[108] Meanwhile, Iraqi Iran-aligned militias began to attack U.S. forces in Iraq.

The Trump Administration, in spite of its bluster, did not muster a strong reaction to these Iranian provocations. Perhaps interpreting this as a sign of weakness, Iran-aligned militias in

---

107   "Iran directly behind tanker attacks off UAE coast, US says," Gulf News, May 25, 2019. (https://gulfnews.com/world/mena/iran-directly-behind-tanker-attacks-off-uae-coast-us-says-1.64179304)

108   David Martin, "Saudi Oil Attack was Approved by Iran's Supreme Leader, U.S. official says". *CBS News*, September 18, 2019.

Iraq intensified attacks on U.S. assets in Iraq, leading Trump to order a retaliatory air strike. At that point, Iran dispatched loyal militias to storm the U.S. Embassy in Baghdad, a major escalation that succeeded in capturing an outer building but failed to breach the main perimeter of the compound. This was the provocation that led Trump to order the drone strike that killed General Soleimani, the Head of the IRGC Quds force, as he arrived in Baghdad in early January 2020.[109]

This move caught the attention of the regime. Seeing that the Trump Administration was not bluffing, it soon ceased its attacks on U.S. forces in Iraq, and made conciliatory gestures to the U.S. It is anyone's guess what could have happened if the "maximum pressure" campaign had been sustained. Instead, Joe Biden was elected President in November 2020, an election that heralded a return of sorts to the foreign policy approach of the Obama era.

Biden, and Pendulum Swings Back

The transition to the Biden Administration led to a return of officials that had been deeply involved in the Obama-era nuclear agreement. As candidate, Biden had vowed to quickly return to the 2015 nuclear deal and to reverse Trump's policy of maximum pressure. In the months that followed, the Biden Administration provided Iran with sanctions relief, in particular allowing Iran to recoup escrowed funds from its oil exports. It also removed Iran's Yemeni proxies, the Houthis, from the U.S. list of foreign terrorist organizations, and somewhat later entertained an Iranian

---

109   Fred Fleitz, "What's Next for Trump's Iran Policy?" *National Review*, June 8, 2020.

demand that the IRGC also be removed from this list, a move that was nevertheless thwarted by an outcry in America.

Meanwhile, the Administration sought to bring back Iran to the negotiating table. Iran issued wide-ranging demands to return to the negotiating table – including the removal of a number of existing sanctions and further financial concessions – which made a return to the nuclear deal increasingly pointless, especially as the sunset dates for its various provisions was fast approaching.

Iran also further raised the stakes by its actions. The U.S. presidential transition, when America was preoccupied by Trump's claims that the election had been stolen – culminating in the assault on the U.S. Capitol on January 6 – Iran realized that it could up the ante. As a result, Iran began enriching uranium to 20 percent (a key step toward making weapons-grade uranium) and by April 2021, it was enriching at 60 percent. Meanwhile, Iran sharply accelerated its targeting of American forces in the Middle East. From January 2021 to March 2023, U.S. Central Command Head Gen. Erik Kurilla testified that U.S. forces had been attacked at almost 80 occasions by Iranian proxies, but that the U.S. responded kinetically only three times.[110]

Sensing a tailwind, the Iranian leadership also dropped pretensions of moderation. In summer 2021, Supreme Leader Khamenei and the IRGC engineered the election of hardliner Ibrahim Raisi as President of Iran – a move interpreted as consolidating authority in preparation for a likely succession to the aging Supreme leader, who was born in 1939. (in 2024, they followed this up by stacking the Assembly of Experts – tasked with

---

110   "American Forces Suffered 78 Iranian Attacks Since 2021: US General," *Al-Arabiya*, March 23, 2023. (https://english.alarabiya.net/News/middle-east/2023/03/23/American-forces-suffered-78-Iranian-attacks-since-2021-US-general)

formally choosing the next Supreme Leader – with hardliners, going so far as excluding former President Rouhani from a seat).

Iran also increased its targeting of neighboring countries. In January 2022, Iranian proxies fired missiles and drone strikes at the UAE capital Abu Dhabi, targeting oil and military installations; two months later, Iranian proxies targeted an oil installation in Saudi Arabia chosen for its proximity to the Saudi Formula One Grand Prix taking place at the time.

Meanwhile, other events threw wrenches into the Biden Administration's efforts to revitalize negotiations with Iran. Russia's full-scale assault on Ukraine in February 2022 diverted attention, but also made the prospect of negotiations harder given Russia's key role in previous negotiation processes. As Iran sided increasingly clearly with Russia and provided weapons for Russia's assault on Ukraine, the prospect of negotiations sank further. The Administration nevertheless sought to find a way forward, in spite of Iranian demands such as the closing of IAEA probes of its undeclared nuclear activities. The "insurmountable political hurdle to further negotiations," in Richard Goldberg's words, only came with the massive protests erupting in Iran following the killing of Mahsa Amini in September 2022.

As a result, the Biden Administration was gradually forced to accept the failure of its efforts to bring back Iran to the negotiating table. But as one analyst put it, "Biden took office with a half-hearted goal of reviving the nuclear deal."[111] Once the prospect of reviving the Iran deal faded, it was not replaced by any other objective, let alone a strategy, aside from seeking to avoid an escalation with Iran or having Iran policy interfere with domestic

---

111 Nahal Toosi, "Has Biden Considered Having an Iran Strategy?" *Politico*, April 16, 2024.

considerations. For example, there is considerable criticism that the Biden Administration has been lax in enforcing oil sanctions on Iran – turning a blind eye to Iran's efforts to create a "ghost fleet" of tankers shipping Iranian crude in ways that circumvent U.S. sanctions. Iranian oil sales to China skyrocketed following Biden's election, indicating that the U.S. was no longer assertively enforcing sanctions – perhaps in the hope of bringing Iran back to the negotiating table. Other considerations may have been to placate China, and to avoid a spike in global oil prices that might result if Iranian oil is taken off the market.[112]

The result has been a reactive and increasingly passive approach to Iran, guided mainly by an urge to avoid escalation and greater U.S. entanglement in the affairs of the region. In retrospect, it is clear that this lack of an active policy emboldened Iran to expand its efforts to establish its dominance in the greater Middle East – as evidenced by its further escalation in 2023-24. After Iranian proxy Hamas attacked southern Israel in October 2024, another proxy – the Houthis – escalated its attacks on commercial shipping in the Red Sea, as well as expanding targets to American and Western warships. Then, in April 2024, Iran further raised the stakes by launching a drone and missile attack directly at Israel for the first time. If Tehran calculated that the U.S. would lean on Israel to prevent an escalation of the conflict, it was correct. While the U.S. and European as well as Arab powers helped shoot down many of the drones and missiles targeting Israel, the U.S. not only refrained from retaliating against Iran – but strongly counseled Israel to engage only in a symbolic retaliation against Iran.

---

112   "How Iran is Boosting Oil Exports Despite US Sanctions," *Deutsche Welle*, January 2, 2023.
(https://www.dw.com/en/how-iran-is-boosting-oil-exports-despite-us-sanctions/a-64562167)

Known Unknowns: The Future of U.S. Iran Policy

Following the U.S. presidential election, the future of U.S. Iran policy was once again in flux in late 2024. The second Trump Administration is expected to lead to a return of hardline policies against Iran. But crucially, from the perspective of regional powers that might be supportive of that, Trump can only stay in power for four years, after which U.S. Iran policy will be anyone's guess. As a result, regional states have been feeling left to their own devices regarding how to deal with Iran's ambitions. Worse, they have been forced to work with other great powers that they perceive to have influence over Tehran.

In Syria, Israel after 2015 accepted the reality that Russia had become a key broker in Syria, particularly as regards its control over large parts of Syria's air space. This meant that if Jerusalem sought to take out Iranian targets in Syria, it would have to ensure that Moscow at a minimum stayed neutral and allowed it to proceed with its operations. This, in turn, meant that Israel has been in no position to join with Western powers in arming Ukraine following Russia's invasion. Similarly, Gulf powers no longer felt able to trust that America would have their backs in the face of the Iranian threat. This led them to seek a limited accommodation with Tehran, in the Saudi case brokered by Beijing in a manner that caught the U.S. unaware.

In sum, Washington's dance with Iran has done serious damage to America's position in the greater Middle East. The U.S. has a long road to go to rebuild the confidence of its partners and allies in the Middle East – and it remains unclear whether this is something the U.S. is even interested in pursuing. In the absence of that, regional powers will make their own calculations.

Among them has been a silver lining: a realignment among the Sunni states, which resulted in great part from a sense that the Sunni civil war was no longer sustainable in the face of American disengagement and relentless Iranian hegemonic ambitions. For the Gulf states, Turkey's turn away from Islamism and a realignment toward nationalism in both domestic and foreign affairs provided an opening that was too good to pass up.

12.

THE FAILURE OF ISLAMISM IN TURKEY RESHUFFLES THE REGION

In the early 2020s, several clear shifts were visible in the geo-politics of the Middle East. With President Trump leaving the White House, the U.S. policy on Iran shifted dramatically, back to the approach taken during the Obama Administration. Iran felt empowered and assertive after having weathered the Trump years, and without U.S. backing, several Gulf states changed track and sought to reduce tensions with Iran. Meanwhile, a major shift took place in Turkey, though this was not immediately visible in President Erdoğan's rhetoric. Under the surface, the Turkish government shifted not so subtly from Islamism to nationalism, leading to a reshuffling of Turkish priorities. The "Brotherhood Axis" was quietly buried, even though Erdoğan's personal dia-tribes sometimes suggested otherwise. This nationalist bent in turn put Turkey on a collision course with Iran both in Syria and in the South Caucasus, further accelerating the rapprochement with the conservative Sunni bloc.

The Failure of Islamism in Turkey

Recep Tayyip Erdogan came to power with the stated intention of making Turkish society more Islamic. He repeatedly spoke of raising "pious generations." As he consolidated power, it became clear that he was serious about this intention. Turkey's religious bureaucracy, the *Diyanet*, grew exponentially in size, surpassing most government ministries and began to issue religious guidance on a variety of issues. Furthermore, the government invested heavily in making the education system more religious. A massive education reform in 2012 paved the way both for increasing the religious content of education in secular schools, and growing the share of religious *imam-hatip* schools compared to the secular ones. These schools were originally intended to produce imams for Turkey's many mosques, but over time developed into a parallel education system, producing millions of students, including girls, who are not allowed to become imams. But *imam-hatip* schools were lavished with funds – in 2018, the government spent double the amount of money per student in religious schools compared to secular schools.[113]

The imam-hatip schools have better facilities and are less cramped than their secular counterparts. Still, they have not succeeded in attracting parents. The reason is simple: religious schools badly underperform other schools in academic quality. Their graduates score much lower on university entrance exams,

---

113   Daren Butler, "With More Islamic Schooling, Erdoğan Aims to Reshape Turkey," *Reuters*, 25 January 2018,

and thus having much lower chances of gaining admission to university programs. As a result, even in religiously conservative areas, Turkish parents have protested the government efforts to transform secular schools into imam-hatip schools. It appears they are more interested in their children's ability to get an education and succeed in the labor market than in raising a pious generation.

The problem goes deeper: even students at imam-hatip schools no longer appear to follow the mold. The Turkish Education Ministry in 2018 issued a report that raised the alarm about the rise of deism among imam-hatip students. Apparently, a not insignificant number of young people found the education in religious schools so unconvincing that they begun to doubt the precepts of Islam. While they did not go so far as to become atheists, they embraced a "deist" approach instead, an individual spirituality decoupled from Islamic principles.[114]

Opinion polls bear out the decline of Islamic observance in Turkey during Erdogan's tenure in power. Between 2001 and 2018, the number of people who reported that religion played a "very important" part in their life declined from 80 to 60 percent. Fasting during the month of Ramadan has declined from 77 to 65 percent. Among young people in particular, religious observance is down – and the phenomenon is particularly clear among the children of the religious middle class that moved into the major cities from the 1970s onward and became the main support base of the AKP.

Many observers have pointed to the irony that religious observance in Turkey grew when the state imposed restrictions

114   Mucahit Bilici, "The Crisis of Religiosity in Turkish Islamism," *Middle East Report*, no. 288, Fall 2018.

on religion, but declined when the state instead began to impose religion on the population. Scholars have shown that this is in fact quite a predictable result of state interference in private matters such as religion, pointing to examples ranging from the United States to Iran to show the negative effect on religiosity of politicization of religion.[115]

In the Turkish case, several factors combined to ensure Erdogan's effort to Islamize Turkey ended in failure. These include technological change, the corruption and clientelism of the regime, and not least the 2016 coup.

Technological change is perhaps the most obvious factor that Erdogan could do very little about. In 2022, 75 percent of Turks were estimated to own a smartphone. The country's youth, therefore, is well-connected and aware of developments in the country and around the world – while obviously being susceptible to the same type of manipulation as smartphone users elsewhere. While Erdogan has been known to say his ideal model of a young person is one with a computer in one hand and a Quran in the other, it seems that young people connected to the world through their smartphones are less inclined to follow religious dogma.

One reason for this is the widespread corruption and clientelism that Erdogan's regime has been associated with. Erdogan's party acronym AK also means "white" in Turkish, a swipe at the corruption of the center-right parties it challenged two decades ago. But few people see the party as pure in any sense. It is telling that the decline of religious belief is particularly visible in the children of the social class closest to the regime itself. And the

---

115   Murat Çokgezen, "Can the State Make you More Religious? Evidence from Turkish Experience," *Journal for the Scientific Study of Religion*, vol. 61 no. 2, 2022.

perhaps most damning indictment of the Erdogan regime is that ideological Islamists have deserted the party. The unreconstructed Islamist Felicity Party was always in opposition to Erdogan, but in recent years made common cause with the opposition Nation Alliance led by the center-left CHP – thus depriving Erdogan of the ability to call his opposition ungodly. Separately, the son of Necmettin Erbakan, the founder of Turkish Islamism, created a breakaway Islamist party of his own in 2018, which began to eat away at the AKP. And Erdogan's former running mate Ahmet Davutoglu broke off to create the Future Party in 2019, allying in parliament with the Felicity Party. Not to be outdone, former Minister of Economy and of Foreign Affairs Ali Babacan, supported by former President Abdullah Gül – both founders of the AKP – broke out to form the center-right DEVA party. None of these parties have had much electoral success, but they are an indication that the AKP increasingly consists of opportunists seeking proximity to power rather than ideologically convinced Islamists.

In addition, twenty years in power has politicized the religious brotherhoods that have historically been so crucial for religious parties to mobilize voters. As one Turkish Islamist told this author when speaking of religious brotherhoods, "they have all become businesses." As the saying goes, power corrupts and absolute power corrupts absolutely – and the visible corruption associated with Erdogan, the regime, and the brotherhoods that support it has seriously compromised the perception of institutionalized religion in the country.

The Rise of Turkish Nationalism

The 2016 failed coup, as mentioned earlier, was a devastating blow to Islamist ideology in Turkey. It was for all practical purposes a civil war within the Turkish state between two wings of the Islamist movement – those led by Erdogan and Fethullah Gülen. The failure of the coup led Gülen's wing to essentially be eradicated, undoing four decades of meticulous efforts to build power within the Turkish state. And while Erdogan emerged victorious and even strengthened his power following the failed coup, it was a hollow victory – because it further drove home the moral bankruptcy of political Islam for millions of Turks. And it deprived Erdogan of an Islamist power base in the bureaucracy, thus forcing him to look elsewhere for support.

As a result, by the end of the 2010s political Islam had run its course in Turkey. In spite of the leadership's best efforts, the rulers appeared to alienate more people from religion than their promotion of religious conservatism managed to attract. In parallel, the composition of the ruling coalitions changed. The rift with the Gülenists deprived Erdogan of his most effective support base within state institutions, who first turned into deadly enemies and were subsequently purged. That in turn left a void in the state that needed to be filled. Significantly, Erdogan had not succeeded in building a loyal constituency large and educated enough to be able to man the bureaucracy. This forced him to turn to the right-wing nationalists that the Gülen-aligned prosecutors had recently targeted.

Several factors facilitated this grand bargain between Erdogan and right-wing nationalists. First, they largely share a common social base of conservative Turks that have a strong nationalist as well as religious identity. Different people may emphasize ethnic or religious aspects of the identity to varying degrees, but since the military began to promote the idea of a "Turkish-Islamic synthesis" in the 1980s, being Muslim and Turkish has come to become largely synonymous for much of the social base of the AKP and the nationalist MHP.

Secondly, the changes in regional affairs discussed in previous chapters brought about a rising sense of nationalism. The nationalist right had opposed Erdogan's outreach to the Kurds and the negotiations with the PKK. Following the rise of the PKK-aligned statelet in northern Syria, the military and intelligence establishment prevailed upon Erdogan to drop this outreach and return to a traditional, hard-core security approach to the Kurdish issue, animated by Turkish nationalism.

New priorities in Turkish Foreign Policy

In the second half of the 2010s, domestic and foreign developments combined to lead to a new turn in Turkish foreign policy. Domestically, Islamism had weakened its hold on society, and nationalism was emerging as the hegemonic ideology in the country. To stay in power, Erdogan was forced to align his rhetoric to a more nationalist discourse. Meanwhile, the Brotherhood-focused foreign policy in the Middle East had turned into an utter failure, isolating Turkey in the region while giving birth to an unlikely alignment of countries – Greece, Cyprus, Israel, Egypt, the UAE, and Saudi Arabia truly make for motley crew that seemed only to have opposition to Turkey in common.

Meanwhile, the AKP government's most fervent Islamist

ideologues had left politics or gone into opposition. This provided a vacuum that the country's security institutions were more
than willing to fill. And the Turkish military and intelligence
bureaucracies were, more than anything else, animated by Turkish
nationalism. These nationalists saw no reason to seek fights with
Saudis or Emiratis, or for that matter with Egyptians and Israelis.
They were not interested in the Sunni Arab Middle East for any
ideological reason. If anything, they harbored a strong disdain for
Iran and its regional ambitions, something that led them view
regional affairs similarly to their Gulf Arab counterparts. And
contrary to Turkey's Islamists, they were very much interested in
their Turkic kin in Azerbaijan and the Central Asian states.

Expanding Turkey's Footprint in the East

During the AKP's first decade in power, Turkey showed relatively little interest in the Caucasus and Central Asia. The AKP
government in 2009-10 embarked on an effort of reconciliation
with Armenia – a complex relationship marred both by ancient
and more recent history. In this endeavor, the AKP government
received the full support of Turkey's liberal intelligentsia, which
had long since been predisposed to a normalization of relations
with Armenia. To Turkey's liberals, acknowledging that a geno-
cide was committed against the Ottoman Empire's Armenian
population in 1915 was an important step in Turkey's democratization, and to that one that would facilitate Turkey's European
integration. But to Turkey's nationalists, normalizing relations
would be unthinkable as long as Armenia continued to occupy

large territories in Azerbaijan, the Turkic country most closely linked with Turkey.

Meanwhile, Turkey's increasingly Islamist policies at home were met with great alarm in Central Asian capitals. All six countries, including Azerbaijan, were firmly committed to a secularist agenda, and much preferred the old, Kemalist Turkey that they had seen as a model.

It should be noted that the Armenian "opening" was not Erdogan's handiwork, but largely run by then-President Abdullah Gül and Foreign Minister Ali Babacan. In fact, Erdogan was the one who stepped in to halt the process once the impact of the initiative on the AKP's nationalist-minded voters began to be seen in polls. This intervention cemented the personal relationship between Erdogan and Azerbaijani President Ilham Aliyev, in spite of the obvious differences in lifestyle and outlook between the highly secular Aliyev family and the Islamist Erdogan.

As Turkey's Middle Eastern adventures led it to become more regionally isolated by 2015 or so, the AKP leadership began paying closer attention to Central Asia and the Caucasus. Both Erdogan and Foreign Minister Davutoğlu became increasingly frequent visitors to regional capitals. But it was toward the end of the 2010s that the shifting priorities came to view. Turkey became a much more active participant in the Council of Turkic-Speaking states – a body that had largely been driven by Azerbaijan and Kazakhstan during the period of Turkey's focus on its Brotherhood agenda in the Middle East.

Turkey's engagement with the region was also aided considerably by the uptick in relations with Uzbekistan following the passing of that country's long-time leader Islam Karimov. A dedicated secularist, Karimov cracked down with an iron fist on expressions of religiosity that he perceived as threatening to Uzbekistan's stability. His successor Shavkat Mirziyoyev adopted a less repressive and more constructive approach to religious matters, all while remaining committed to the secular nature of the state. This opened up for a rapid improvement of relations: Erdogan visited Tashkent for the first time in 13 years in November 2016, only weeks after Karimov's demise.

Meanwhile, Central Asian leaders began to take note of Turkey's possible role as counterbalancing force to Russian influence. Turkish-Russian relations were on a rollercoaster in the mid-2010s as the two powers clashed in Syria. Turkey's shootdown of a Russian jet along the Syrian border in 2015 was a major event, which nevertheless led to Russia slapping sanctions on Turkey that hurt the Turkish economy significantly. While Turkey eventually had to apologize for that event, it found itself in proxy conflict with Russia in Syria as well as in Libya. Then came the 2020 war between Armenia and Azerbaijan.

The conflict between Armenia and Azerbaijan had heated up throughout the 2010s, as Armenia's approach grew increasingly uncompromising – Armenian leaders began referring to occupied territories in Azerbaijan as "liberated" territories, sponsored the settlement of ethnic Armenians from the Middle East in these territories, and the defense minister even spoke of "new wars for new territories." The 2018 velvet revolution that brough Nikol Pashinyan to power initially seemed to augur well for the peace process, as Pashinyan was, unlike his two predecessors, not from Karabakh and initially appeared interested in seeking a negotiated settlement. But as Pashinyan came under pressure from nationalist groups, his rhetoric grew even harsher than that of his predecessors.

Not staying at harsh rhetoric against Azerbaijan, Armenia also provoked Turkey's ire by staging large commemorations of the hundredth anniversary of the defunct 1920 Treaty of Sèvres, which would have created an Armenian state on large parts of present-day Turkey's territory. Armenia's President mentioned that the Treaty, while never implemented, remains "in force" – thus laying territorial claims on Turkey.[116] Former Armenian National Security Adviser Gerard Libaridian defined the statement as a "declaration of at least diplomatic war" on Turkey.[117]

Ankara may have seen it as more than diplomatic. In retrospect, it appears this was the point at which the Turkish leadership decided to back Azerbaijan's aim to restore its authority over the areas of Azerbaijan that had been occupied by Armenia since 1994. Turkish weapons sales to Baku shot through the roof over summer 2020, and the two countries organized large-scale military exercises in early August. Crucially, Turkey left several F-16 fighter jets in Azerbaijan following these exercises, a clear deterrent against any external power – be it Russia or Iran – that would have considered intervening to stop Azerbaijan's military operation.

That operation, which led to the 44-day war in October-November 2020, featured the use of advanced Turkish and Israeli military technology that Armenian forces, in the absence of a Rus-

---

116   "President Armen Sarkissian: "The Treaty of Sèvres even today remains an essential document for the right of the Armenian people to achieve a fair resolution of the Armenian issue", President.am, August 10, 2020.

117   Gerard Libaridian, "A Step, This Time a Big Step, Backwards," Aravot, September 1, 2020.

sian intervention, were unable to answer. A Russian-negotiated cease-fire deal was announced on November 9, ushering in a new reality in the South Caucasus that for the first time since independence featured another outside power as an important security guarantor. This reality – with Turkey emerging as a power in the post-Soviet space – was codified in June 2021 through the Shusha Declaration, a mutual defense treaty between Turkey and Azerbaijan.

These developments were duly noted in Central Asian capitals. Particularly after the Russian invasion of Ukraine in February 2022, Central Asian states and particularly Kazakhstan and Uzbekistan began fast-tracking the expansion of military and intelligence cooperation with Turkey, all while expanding their defense spending. They also began developing defense cooperation with one another, with the Azerbaijani-Uzbek cooperation expanding rapidly alongside the already existing Azerbaijani-Kazakh and Uzbek-Kazakh relations.

Also in 2021, Turkic cooperation took a new step as the Turkic Council was upgraded to a full international organization, the Organization of Turkic States. This new body is becoming an important feature of regional affairs, playing a visible role in the diplomacy of both Turkey, Azerbaijan and the Central Asian states. Obviously, the OTS is competing with Russian-led and Chinese-led programs in the wider Central Asian area, and it remains to be seen whether Turkey has the wherewithal to keep expanding its influence in Central Asia in a meaningful way, without triggering active efforts by Beijing or Moscow to counter it.

Still, the expansion of Turkish interests eastward indicate just how much Turkish foreign policy has changed in a decade.

From seeking to support the creation of a Muslim Brotherhood-based network of power across the Middle East, Turkey is now focusing on development an alliance with secularist governments in the Caucasus and Central Asia. This has won Turkey new friends, and relieved its problems with some powers – but it has also put it on collision course with others – most notably Iran.

Clashing with Iran in Syria and the Caucasus

Before the Arab Upheavals, Erdogan's government had put considerable effort into a rapprochement with Iran. While Turkey's Islamists are strongly Sunni and harbor traditional skepticism of Shi'a Iran, the Brotherhood ideology that influence Turkish Islamism was considerably more pro-Iranian. And following the 1979 Islamic revolution, Turkish Islamists adopted largely positive views of Iran. During Khomeini's lifetime in particular, Tehran's efforts to export the revolution had a wide-ranging impact on Turkish Islamism.

Although traditional Turkish Islamic milieus typically viewed the Iranian Shi'a as deviant and schismatic, Islamist thinkers after 1979 emphasized and repeated the Khomeini regime's pan-Islamist rhetoric emphasizing the political importance of *Ummah* – the worldwide community of Muslims. When Erbakan's Welfare Party grew to prominence in the 1990s, a large number of its cadres had been profoundly influenced by the ideological defenders of the Iranian revolution. By 2001, when the AKP was formed as the successor to the Welfare Party, pro-Islamic Revolution leaders were of an age that allowed them to exercise greater political and ideological influence over Turkish Islamist and Islamic thought as a whole.

During the AKP's time in power, its leadership up to 2011 showed considerable deference to Iran, and, at times, actively worked to court Tehran. Iran saw Turkish-American controversies over the Iraq war as an opportunity to step forward and ingratiate itself to Turkey. By the mid-2000s, more than 50 percent of Turks viewed Iran favorably, while percentages of those who held positive views of the U.S. were in the single digits.[118] This gave Erdoğan a freer hand to take the relationship with Iran to another level, while he gradually dismantled Turkey's historically close relationship with Israel. Remarkably, in this period Turkey became a defender of Iran's nuclear program as well as an apologist for the Iran regime's brutal suppression of the 2009 "Green Revolution."[119]

Erdoğan and his foreign minister Davutoğlu went from seeking to mediate between Iran and the West on the nuclear issue to becoming outspoken defenders of Iran's nuclear program – Erdoğan, for example, urged world powers possessing nuclear weapons to abolish their own arsenals before meddling with Iran, and frequently drew the analogy to Israel's nuclear arsenal.[120] This approach was in part a result of the Pan-Islamic thinking of leading AKP intellectuals like Davutoğlu. In his academic work, Davutoğlu urged Turkey and other Muslim societies to work for Islamic unity. Erdoğan and Davutoğlu long viewed

---

118   Daphne McCurdy, "Turkish-Iranian Relations: When Opposites Attract," *Turkish Policy Quarterly*, vol. 7, no. 2, 2008.

119   Eric Edelman, Svante E. Cornell, Aaron Lobel, Michael Makovsky, *The Roots of Turkish Conduct*, Washington: Bipartisan Policy Center, 2013. http://silkroadstudies.org/resources/pdf/publications/1312BPC.pdf.

120   "Erdoğan: Kimse İsrail'deki nükleer silahların hesabını sormuyor," T24.com.tr, March 30, 2012, https://t24.com.tr/haber/erdogan-kimse-israildeki-nukleer-silahlarin-hesabini-sormuyor,200555

Iran as a potential partner that should be brought on board with Turkey's efforts to build Islamic solidarity and reshape the Middle East. Meanwhile, Ankara was actively seeking to establish itself as a senior partner to the Assad regime in Syria – an apparent contradiction given that regime's dependence on Iran.

More material considerations were also at play. Turkish-Iranian commercial relations stretch deeply into the Turkish Islamist movement, including senior figures close to Erdoğan. The reach of Iran's tentacles into Turkey were evident in the major Iran-Turkey oil-for-gold scandal involving Iranian gold trader Reza Zarrab. An indictment in the United States District Court for the Second District of New York charged that Iranian efforts to circumvent and violate U.S. sanctions, spearheaded by Zarrab, involved multi-million dollar bribes to several key members of Erdoğan's cabinet and extended to influential officials in Turkish state-owned banks.[121]

From 2011 onwards, however, growing sectarian violence in the Middle East again changed the Turkish Islamist movement's view of Iran. While the AKP peddled a pan-Islamic approach built on seeking consensus among Muslims against western influence and "colonialism," it was confronted with Iran's resolute, uncompromising and Shi'a sectarian approach.

Turkey's reckoning with Iran would unfold in Syria. While Turkish leaders after 2011 saw the Sunni majority's rise to power (represented by the Muslim Brotherhood) as both unavoidable and desirable, Iran provided the regime with the option of full-scale repression. Iran not only endorsed but actively supported the

---

121   United States District Court, Southern District of New York, Superseding Indictment, S4 14 Cr. 867 (RMB), https://www.justice.gov/usao-sdny/press-release/file/994976/download.

Syrian regime's brutal repression, which led to the flight of several million Syrians to Turkey.

The Iranian regime and its client militias then established a corridor linking Tehran to the Mediterranean Sea across Iraq. Meanwhile, Turkish-supported Brotherhood-led forces proved incompetent on the battlefield, forcing Ankara to rely increasingly on radical militias, including Al Qaeda-aligned groups like Jabhat al-Nusra. But beginning in 2018, Ankara doubled down on its involvement in Syria by inserting its own troops into the country's north, with a view to create a permanent Turkish zone of influence. This further deepened its relationship with Sunni Islamist militias, which now functioned as Turkish proxies. In 2019, Turkey also became directly involved in fighting against the Assad regime. As a result, the Turkish Islamist government found itself in a proxy war against Iran's Islamist government. In February 2020, over 30 Turkish troops were killed by Syrian forces, leading to a massive Turkish retaliatory attack that targeted both Syrian regime and Hezbollah forces. Given Iran's presence on the ground in Syria, this risked bringing the two powers in direct confrontation, while Turkey also targeted Russian materiel and came into conflict with Russian proxy forces.

The intensity of Turkey's intervention in northern Syria was unprecedented. Less than six months later, Turkey's endorsement of Azerbaijan's operation to restore control over its occupied territories also worsened relations with Iran. Fearful of Azerbaijani separatism inside Iran, the Tehran regime had developed into Armenia's most reliable sponsor and supporter on the international scene. Furthermore, for Iran, Armenia served as a convenient wedge separating Turkey from the rest of the Turkic world.

But after the 2020 44-day war, Turkey and Azerbaijan insisted on the inclusion of a clause in the cease-fire agreement that envisaged a transport corridor being created through southern Armenia, in order to link Azerbaijan to its exclave Nakhichevan and onward to Turkey. Armenia and Azerbaijan disagreed on the nature of this corridor, with Azerbaijan demanding extra-territorial control over it – something that in turn would jeopardize Iran's access to Armenia.

Tensions rose further in September 2022 as Azerbaijan and Armenia clashed over undemarcated parts of their common border. Azerbaijan gained control over higher ground that provided it with an advantageous position for a possible military operation targeting southern Armenia. Only a month later, the Iranian Revolutionary Guards ground forces launched large-scale military exercises on the Iranian border with Azerbaijan. These exercises included staging amphibious operations to cross the Araxes River, thus simulating an Iranian ground invasion of Azerbaijan. They were paired with Iranian warnings to Azerbaijan concerning the creation of a Zangezur corridor, and threats to curtail the country's military and security cooperation with Israel.[122]

Two months later, Turkey and Azerbaijan staged the largest military exercises to date on the northern side of the Iran-Azerbaijan border. Ankara and Baku also practiced amphibious crossings of the Araxes, and pointed to the modern nature of their weaponry, which contrasted sharply with the antiquated equipment used by the Iranian military. Furthermore, the exercises were supervised by the Turkish Defense Minister as well as the Turk-

---

122   Aziza Goyushzade, "Iran Holds Military Exercises on Border Amid Tensions with Azerbaijan," Voice of America, October 20, 2022.

ish chief of general staff. This served as a further indication that Turkey now openly challenged Moscow's security dominance in the South Caucasus and sent a clear signal to Iran that Turkey was serious about its security commitment to Azerbaijan. In addition, Baku and Ankara both intimated that the exercises were part of the integration of the military forces of the two countries. While Azerbaijani and Turkish officials had long paid allegiance to the concept of "one nation, two states" to emphasize the closeness of the two people, they now added a third: "one army."[123]

Meanwhile, Turkey was beginning to crack down on Iranian intelligence operations on its soil – numerous Iranian dissidents, including high-profile figures, had been abducted or attacked in Turkey. While Ankara in earlier times had handled such incidents discreetly, it now televised busts of Iranian spy rings. Turkish intelligence even proceeded to public media briefings on Iranian intelligence activity and its efforts to thwart it.[124]

Turkey and Iran are thus locked in a rivalry both in Syria and in the Caucasus, with frequent differences of opinion on Iraqi affairs as well. This souring of relations occurred in parallel with a normalization of Turkish relations with Sunni Arab powers, another major shift in Turkish foreign policy.

Making up with the Arabs

As a result of its support for Islamist regime change across the Middle East, Turkey found itself increasingly isolated in the

---

123   Cavid Veliyev, "Azerbaijan-Türkiye military cooperation: One nation, one army," *Daily Sabah*, December 23, 2022.

124   Maryam Sinayee, "Turkish Intelligence Briefs Media On 'Iranian Kidnap Plot'," Iran International, February 12, 2022. (https://www.iranintl.com/en/202202128669)

aftermath of the overthrow of the Brotherhood regime in Egypt in 2013. As we have seen, Turkey aligned with Qatar and invested heavily in preventing the UAE, Saudi Arabia and Egypt from succeeding in their effort to have would-be strongman Khalifa Haftar take control over Libya. Yet as Turkey's internal balances shifted in a nationalist direction, and the zealous pursuit of a Brotherhood axis faded, priorities also changed. The Turkish security establishment saw little reason to extend its spat with the Emiratis and Saudis, or in fact to antagonize Egypt and Israel. More likely, they saw these controversies as unnecessary distractions, particularly as Turkish views of Iran soured and regional balances changed.

However, several factors extended the cold war within the Sunni camp. First, Turkish leaders were in lash out-mode following the failed 2016 coup. They drew a direct connection between the 2013 coup in Egypt, the 2016 coup against Erdogan, and subsequently the blockade of Qatar. To Turkish leaders, these were not separate events but part of a grand conspiracy to undermine the Turkish-led axis in the Middle East. President Erdogan's reaction to the 2019 ouster of long-time Sudanese leader Omar Al-Bashir is indicative: Erdogan commented that the ouster was "directed against Turkey." While this would seem an outlandish statement, Erdogan felt that the ouster was directed against his long-time ally. Turkey in 2018 had begun to develop Suakin island, on the Red Sea, with the support of Qatar, a move that was not well received in Saudi Arabia. As such, the logic went, Riyadh and Abu Dhabi had an interest in ousting Bashir to prevent Turkey from developing a military presence in Suakin and the Red Sea.[125]

---

125   Dorian Jones, "Analysts: Ouster of Sudanese Leader Hurts Ankara's Regional Goals," Voice of America, April 29, 2019.

Turkish leaders in particular blamed Egypt and the UAE for supporting the Gulen movement. The Saudi and Emirati-led blockade of Qatar in 2017 deepened the conflict for some time, and the inclusion of demands that Qatar close down the Turkish military presence in the country strengthened the sense in Ankara that the blockade targeted Turkey's rise a regional power. Of course, in 2018, the fallout of the Khashoggi murder further delayed any process of normalization between Turkey and the Gulf monarchies.

Several factors led Turkey to reverse itself from 2020 onward. First, the election of Biden reshuffled the region as it was perceived to lessen pressures on Iran to advance its hegemonic agenda. By that time, Turkey had turned sufficiently against Iran that it was concerned that this changed balance of power would embolden Iran – thus strengthening the logic of finding common ground with the Arab monarchies. Second, Turkey's economy was in dire straits at the time. The lira had depreciated perilously against the dollar and Euro, with costs of living going through the roof. In 2019, the AKP lost the mayoral elections in both Istanbul and Ankara, something that emboldened Turkey's opposition and led to flashing red lights in the Presidential palace concerning the crucial presidential elections set for 2023.

With Western investment declining, Turkey needed capital to keep the economy afloat – and just relying on Qatar would not be sufficient. As a result, the pragmatic side of Erdogan understood that a rapprochement with the Sunni Arab powers was now necessary. Meanwhile, the state establishment and Erdogan's nationalist allies in government had long worked to suppress the ideological element in Turkish foreign policy. To them, Turkey now suffered from the alignment of forces generated by its ill-fated ideological foray. In this respect, the Abraham Accords of August 2020 were a game-changer. While Erdogan initially lashed out at the Arab states that signed accords with Israel, the Accords confirmed that the alignment countering Turkey's regional ambitions was solidifying. First, the creation of the Eastern Mediterranean Gas Forum had indicated this, and now the start of formal relations between several Arab states and Israel consolidated it.

As a result, from 2021 onward Turkey was ready to recalibrate its rhetoric. It received a major boost from the January 2021 Al-Ula summit, in which the Gulf states and Qatar arrived at a reconciliation and normalization of relations. The timing of this agreement – coinciding with the transfer of power from Trump to Biden – was no coincidence. The Gulf monarchies saw an urgent need to resolve their problems in an environment where they may be left to deal with Iran on their own. The deal allowed Turkey to open relations with the Gulf monarchies without appearing to let down its ally Qatar. In fact, the deal instead provided Turkey with a rationale to appear to support a constructive process in the region.

Erdogan now took on a much more constructive tone in his speeches, and sought to reach out to the Gulf Arab states in order to reduce tensions and reinvigorate economic ties. In doing so, however, Ankara ran into a problem. Given Erdogan's aversion to Sisi, Turkey tried to focus on reaching out to the UAE and Saudi Arabia, leaving out Egypt – which offered little economic incentive. But Turkish leaders were met with a resolute response: improve relations with all of us, or none. Reluctantly, Turkey complied.

Its efforts to rebuild relations with Abu Dhabi bore fruit in late 2021, when the Emirati Crown Prince Mohammed bin Zayed visited Turkey and announced a $10 billion investment deal. On the Saudi front, Erdogan agreed to remove the main irritant in bilateral relations by transferring the Khashoggi murder case to Saudi jurisdiction. After visiting Jeddah in April 2022, Erdogan on his return ordered the closure of the Brotherhood-aligned Mekameleen television station, which operated from Turkish soil and sought to beam Brotherhood propaganda into Egypt.

Ankara had for some time asked the Egyptian Brotherhood activists in the country to downplay their rhetoric, but this step was a symbolic indication of Turkey's change of heart. Also in early 2022, Turkey asked the members of Hamas's military wing, the al-Qassam brigades, to leave the country – while continuing to allow Hamas political leaders to stay.[126] These steps in turn allowed for improvement of relations with both Israel and Egypt. In the latter case, the process was slow and suffered numerous bumps, but Erdogan finally shook hands with his erstwhile nemesis in Qatar during the 2022 World Cup, and finally visited Cairo in February 2024.

Implications

On the eve of Hamas's horrific October 7 pogrom in southern Israel, the Middle East appeared to have settled into a more predictable, traditional balance. The three-way competition between

---

126   Baruch Yedid, "Turkey to Expel Members of Hamas' Military Wing – Report," Jewishpress. com, February 17, 2022.

Iran, the radical Sunni group, and the conservative Sunni group appeared to be over. Instead, a newfound if sometimes reluctant alignment was emerging among the Sunni powers, in which the threat of Iran's regional ambition loomed large.

This new balance even held the promise of a larger break-through: Saudi Arabia joining the Abraham Accords and opening full diplomatic and economic relations with Israel. Such a development – codifying and expanding a relationship that already had strengthened behind the scenes – would have been a major blow to Iran's effort to build its hegemonic position in the region. It would have augured well for the ability of regional states to check Iran's ambitions even in the absence of a strong American commitment to do so.

Perhaps, this shift was one reason that prompted the attack of October 7. Those attacks forced Israel to respond by seeking to eliminate Hamas in Gaza. Because of Gaza's urban geography and Hamas's willful use of human shields, such an operation would by necessity generate large civilian casualties. That would in turn put serious pressure on the newfound alignment among Sunni monarchies, Turkey and Israel – and all but rule out any Saudi-Israeli normalization in the short turn.

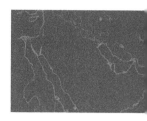

13.
DEALING WITH IRAN IN A POST-ISLAMIST MIDDLE EAST? IMPLICATIONS FOR AMERICAN POLICY

A reader of the preceding chapters could be forgiven for concluding that the Greater Middle East is a hopeless morass of problematic states with capricious leaders, in a region dominated by Islamist ideology that portrays America as enemy number one. The twists and turns of Middle East geopolitics are so frequent and so numerous that it would appear difficult for the United States to devise a policy to deal with them constructively.

Yet the tragic events of the last few years should put an end to the notion that America could just up and leave, leaving the regional powers of the Greater Middle East to "share the neighborhood" with each other, as one American official once suggested. Even though the challenge posed by China is indisputably the most serious matter confronting American national security in coming decades, in an era of great power competition, everything is connected. America faces an alignment of revisionist powers that have made common cause to roll back America's role in the world. To illustrate, America's unwieldy departure from Afghanistan helped trigger Vladimir Putin's decision to attack Ukraine.[127] Iran then rapidly moved to supply Russia with ammunition, ballistic missiles and drones. China not only buys almost 90 percent of Iran's oil, transported by a growing "dark fleet" of tankers. Beijing actively supports Iran, and in parallel with its growing proximity to Tehran in recent years, China (like Russia) has become increasingly antagonistic to Israel– an antagonism that it exports back to America itself through the bias of the wildly popular Chinese-owned Tiktok application. The three powers now regularly hold joint military exercises, as happened in the Gulf of Oman in March 2024, indicating the emergence of a strategic coalition to counter the America-led West. And in October 2023, in great part to stop America's attempt to achieve a normalization of relations between Israel and Saudi Arabia, Iran helped plan and execute Hamas's horrific terrorist attack on southern Israel. Many other examples could be mentioned.

If the U.S. would heed the call to leave the Middle East to its own devices, the result would not be a region "shared" by regional powers. Instead, the region would almost certainly fall under the spell of America's adversaries. As the past several years have shown, Iran's adversaries are only capable of standing up to Tehran when backed by the muscle provided by the United

---

127   Russian Security Council head Nikolay Patrushev remarked already in August
       2021 that "a similar situation awaits those who are banking on America in
       Ukraine." Weeks after, Russia began moving troops and tanks to the Ukrainian
       border. See Carl Bildt, "Did the Afghan Failure Lead to the Ukraine War?" *Project
       Syndicate*, August 16, 2022. (https://www.project-syndicate.org/commentary/
       afghanistan-us-failure-set-stage-for-russia-invasion-ukraine-by-carl-bildt-2022-08)

States. In the absence of American leadership, regional states will have little alternative but to seek a rapprochement with Tehran. Understanding that Iran could threaten the Kingdom's entire modernization program after Iran conducted strikes on its oil infrastructure at Abqaiq, Saudi Arabia went to China to seek mediation with Iran, leading to a March 2023 agreement.

Leaving the Middle East to the tenders mercies of America's antagonists will not be devoid of cost. There is no doubt that other countries' leaders are watching America's vacillation in the Middle East. This is the case particularly for powers that maintain at least one leg in the Western-led international system, such as India, Turkey, and the Central Asian states. If the leaders of these states see America retreating from the Middle East, an area that has been central to American foreign policy for decades, it is likely that they will make other calculations – and play nice with the emerging revisionist axis linking Beijing, Moscow and Tehran. Recent reports indicate that Arab Gulf states now have begun restricting U.S. use of their territory to target Iranian proxies – an indication that they are betting that détente with Iran is more likely to help avoid Iranian strikes on their infrastructure than their partnership with the United States.

Thus, America cannot counter China by leaving the Middle East to its own devices. Doing so would only empower Russia, China and Iran to assert hegemony over Eurasia as a whole. That in turn would undermine America's ability to maintain freedom of navigation and the openness of international trade, and reduce America's ability to influence world affairs.

What, then, are the principles that should guide America's approach to the Greater Middle East? A starting point is that

America has one key adversary in the region. While it may not have any true friends in the region, (with the exception of Israel) it does have a number of actual or potential partners who can be influenced to cooperate with American priorities.

America's key adversary is the Islamic Republic of Iran. Over almost half a century, the regime has shown over and over again that antagonism toward the United States is hardwired into its *raison d'etre*. It would be only a slight exaggeration to state that if the "Great Satan" did not exist, the Iranian mullahs would have to invent it. Yet Iranian diplomats and negotiators are skilled; and over time, they have proven remarkably astute in generating confusion about the regime's intention. When it has suited its purposes, the regime has indicated a willingness to make a tactical retreat. For example, Tehran indicated a willingness to cooperate with America against Al Qaeda following September 11, while the regime in reality harbored Al Qaeda fighters both before and after the attacks. Similarly, when confronted with American pressure, the regime has shown its ability to influence America's debate on the region to increase Washington's willingness to negotiate with Tehran – as indicated by the revelation of an "Iran Experts Initiative" masterminded by former foreign minister Javad Zarif to influence Western thinking on Iran.[128] And as seen in preceding chapters, the drive to seek an arrangement with Iran has repeatedly clouded not just the worldview of American officials, but led them to ignore facts about Iran's actions – such as Washington's refusal to see the extent of Iran's role behind the Houthis in Yemen. Throughout, Iran has single-mindedly advanced its ambitions of hegemony across the Greater

128   Jay Solomon, "Inside Iran's Influence Operation," *Semafor*, September 29, 2023. (https://www.semafor.com/article/09/25/2023/inside-irans-influence-operation)

Middle East. It has done so doggedly and successfully, in spite of enormous domestic and regional constraints.

Of course, America has other issues in the Middle East to attend to. Depending on one's viewpoint, these could include Arab-Israeli peace, the rebuilding of ravaged states like Syria and Yemen, and the promotion of human rights and democracy. But practically all major issues confronting the United States have in common the nefarious role of Iran. One partial exception is the role of Salafi-Jihadi extremism, the rise of which at times, such as during the rise of ISIS, provided Washington and Tehran with a common enemy. But even here, Iran looms large. As the Saudi Crown Prince has acknowledged, the support for Salafi extremism was an ill-conceived reaction to the Iranian revolution; as for the rise of ISIS, it was a result in part of a decision by the Assad regime, an Iranian proxy, to release Sunni jihadi terrorists from Syrian prisons. And Iran's support for Hamas and dalliance with Al Qaeda shows its willingness to embrace Sunni extremists when it suits its purposes.

It is therefore imperative that America's Middle East policy be guided by the primary objective of confronting Iran and working to roll back Iranian influence across the region. The question is, how can this be achieved?

First, it is no longer sustainable for Washington to have pendulum swings between engagement and confrontation with Iran. To succeed, America will need to have consistency in its Iran policy that exceeds the length of a presidential term. Even if one supports the notion of negotiations with Iran, these will have little expectation of success if their result is likely to be voided by the next American administration. And as the Trump presidency's "maximum pressure" campaign showed, a policy focusing on confrontation is unlikely to yield results if Tehran can just hold on until the next presidential election and expect pressure to dissipate.

Second, America must approach its partners in the region with the goal of countering Iran being at the center of its attention. For this purpose, Saudi Arabia and the Gulf monarchies are obviously key players. This, however, is a relationship that has been mismanaged. When Saudi Arabia was truly a source of extremism across the Middle East and beyond, the U.S. kept close relations with the Kingdom. When the Kingdom embarked on a process of modernization and purged the supporters of Salafi-Jihadi extremism from its governing bodies, relations with America deteriorated. There is a reason for this: the unconscionable murder of Muslim Brotherhood activist and journalist Jamal Khashoggi in the Saudi consulate in Istanbul. But the U.S. must be able to rank its priorities and keep several goals in mind at the same time. While this was a gruesome and unjustifiable act, it led Washington to completely ignore the Saudi government's remarkable process of rolling back extremist interpretations of Islam in Saudi society as well as in Saudi foreign policy. While this was done mainly through authoritarian means, it is already beginning to have a visible effect worldwide, in the deflation of the Sunni jihadist threat. Unfortunately, the U.S. stance on Saudi Arabia prevented America from keeping its eye on the prize: to roll back Iranian influence, for which the downgrading of relations with Saudi Arabia was simply an act of diplomatic malpractice. It did nothing to achieve the goals of domestic transformation that America sought in Saudi Arabia, and undermined America's standing in the region at large. In Tehran, the mullahs must have laughed and shook their heads at America's folly.

The U.S. must also organize its Turkey policy in accordance with its key priorities in the Middle East, this time reconciling them with its priorities in Eastern Europe. Given that Iran and Russia have joined forces, the logic is straightforward. While Turkey is a problematic ally in many ways, its role is absolutely crucial in countering the regional influence of Russia and Iran. This means that America should work diligently to remove irritants in the relationship. Some of these are on the Turkish side, and are matters Washington can hardly influence – such as the conspiracist worldview of the Turkish elite and the anti-American and anti-Semitic reflexes of President Erdoğan. But at the very least, America should try not to confirm and amplify these conspiracist views. In the case of Syria, Washington has blatantly failed to do so. Its support for the Syrian Kurdish YPG may have been understandable in the heat of the struggle against ISIS. In the years since, the U.S. has doubled down on what it initially termed a "temporary" arrangement. In so doing, the U.S. has effectively sacrificed its relationship with a major NATO ally that could function as a leading counterbalance to both Iran and Russia – for the sake of rag-tag Marxist-Leninist militia group that is part of an organization the U.S. itself considers a terrorist group. The strategic logic of this choice is difficult to discern. While the road to a reconstructed relationship with Turkey is long and arduous, there is no alternative but to walk that road.

Obviously, the Greater Middle East consists of more states than Saudi Arabia and Turkey, and many of these are important pieces of the puzzle in an American strategy to contain Iran.

And emphasizing the importance of these states does not mean that Washington should give either a blank check to pursue policies that are counter-productive, like Riyadh's war in Yemen or Turkey's gunboat diplomacy in the Mediterranean. The U.S. should continue to seek to influence the decisions of the Saudi and Turkish elites through both carrots and sticks. But in doing so, it must keep the long-term strategic goal in mind. This means that the U.S. should make a serious effort to establish a long-term strategic partnership with these countries to counter the Iranian threat – and work for the coordination of efforts between them.

As we have seen in recent years, the spat between the Turkish-led and Saudi-led coalitions over ideological matters in the wake of the Arab upheavals only benefited Iran. Now that Turkey has changed its foreign policy approach, it has come to clash with Iran in both the Caucasus and Syria, indicating that the prospect of building a counter-Iran coalition is stronger than ever.

What, then, should be the goal of such a policy, and what tools should be deployed to help achieve that goal? Defining this must start with the recognition that it is late in the game. Iran is on the brink of nuclear breakout, and is feeling bold enough not only to mastermind the October 7 attacks but to target Israel directly with a barrage of missiles and drones. Not staying at that, the Iranian regime has plotted to assassinate high-level former U.S. officials as well as Iranian dissidents on American soil. Meanwhile, the regime's standing at home is precarious. Iran approaches a succession to Supreme Leader Khamenei, and the regime is able to remain in power only through the deployment of brute force on a large scale.

Against this background, the end goal for American policy must be to change the nature of the regime; an intermediate goal must be to change the behavior of the regime. American attempts to engineer regime change, as in Iraq, have met with utter failure, and few today suggest a military operation to topple the regime. But particularly in the post-Khamenei period, there is likely to be a shift in the nature of the regime, with many observers pointing to the likelihood of a declining role for the clergy and an enhanced role of the military, as well as the IRGC. It is in America's interest to position itself in such a way as to influence the calculations of Khamenei's successors. Even in the interim, experience shows that when met with overwhelming force and a determined opponent, the Iranian regime – in the interest of self-preservation – will back down. But there is only likely to be a shift in the regime's behavior and nature if Iranian decision-makers see this as the least risky option. Up to now, that has not been the case.

At this point one must take a step back and ponder whether the Greater Middle East will forever be a region of threats and dangers to the United States, or whether there may be an upside, a light at the end of the tunnel. The upheavals of the past decades suggest there might be. As this volume has sought to show, the most negative driving force across the region in the past half-century has been the rise to prominence of Islamist ideology. But there is much to indicate that Islamism may have peaked, and is now in decline. Exhibit one is Saudi Arabia, once the epicenter of extremist Salafism. Driven by the yearnings of a younger generation of Saudis, Crown Prince Muhammad bin Salman took a sledgehammer to the country's retrograde forces. Openly embracing a return to "moderate Islam," the Crown Prince has faced relatively little opposition. While he has used authoritarian methods to roll back the religious establishment, public opinion polls show a growing proportion of Saudis across different generations embracing the turn away from extremism.

Similarly in Turkey, political Islam is clearly on the decline. While it was the most powerful and ascendant force in society for decades, under Erdoğan Turkish society has become more, not less secular. In parallel, a new political equilibrium has formed pulling Turkey in a more nationalist direction. And in Iran itself, the mullahs have similarly failed to keep religion alive. Tales have long been told of empty mosques across Iran, but there is now survey data showing the extent of Iran's secularization.[129] Less than a third of Iranians identified as Shi'ite Muslims, and almost half reported having gone from religious to non-religious during their lifetime. While Khamenei maintains control through force, future Iranian leaders will likely be compelled however reluctantly, just as Erdoğan has been, to shift away from Islamist ideology as the glue holding the ruling elite together.

It is obviously too early to declare Islamism a spent force. It is noticeably stronger in place where Islamists have not been in government, and Islamists continue to command many young men with guns.

Still, the contours of a post-Islamist Middle East are beginning to emerge on the horizon. That has large implications for American interests. It would not suddenly make the region

---

129   Pooyan Tamimi Arab and Ammar Maleki, "Iran's Secular Shift: New Survey Reveals Huge Changes in Religious Beliefs," *the Conversation*, September 10, 2020. (https://theconversation.com/irans-secular-shift-new-survey-reveals-huge-changes-in-religious-beliefs-145253)

an EU-like area of peace and harmony, as the replacement of Islamism with nationalism, the likely outcome in most countries, could continue to generate conflict and discord. And it would not resolve the deep and chronic problems of governance and corruption that plague the region as a whole. But it would mean that an ideology that is fundamentally anti-American would no longer be dominant across the region. In turn, it could reduce the hostility of Middle Eastern societies toward the West as a whole and the U.S. in particular. And for American foreign policy, it would mean that the Middle East might not just be an area replete with fires to put out and dragons to slay – but one that could play a normal role in world affairs and where American interests can switch to positive agendas like economic growth and development. In order to get to such a rosy scenario, however, America must first figure out the Iran problem.

ABOUT THE AUTHOR

SVANTE E. CORNELL is Research Director of the American Foreign Policy Council's Central Asia-Caucasus Institute in Washington D.C., and a co-founder of the Institute for Security and Development Policy in Stockholm, Sweden. Cornell was educated at the Middle East Technical University and Uppsala University. He formerly served as Associate Professor at Uppsala University and at Johns Hopkins-University-SAIS, and is also a Policy Advisor with the Jewish Institute for National Security of America and a member of the Royal Swedish Academy of War Sciences.